Canadian Girls Who Rocked the World

*I hope you rock
the world one day!*

Canadian Girls Who Rocked the World

Tanya Lloyd

Illustrations by Joanna Clark

Whitecap Books
Vancouver / Toronto

Edited by Elizabeth McLean
Proofread by Elizabeth Salomons
Cover illustration and design by Rose Cowles
Interior design by Margaret Lee / Bamboo & Silk Design Inc.

Printed and bound in Canada.

National Library of Canada Cataloguing in Publication Data

Lloyd, Tanya, 1973–
    Canadian girls who rocked the world

    Includes index.
    ISBN 1-55285-203-2

    1. Teenage girls—Canada—Biography—Juvenile literature. 2. Women—
Canada—Biography—Juvenile literature. 3. Teenage girls—Canada—attitudes.
I. Title.
FC26.W6L56 2001   j305.235'092271   C2001-910266-6
CT3270.L56 2001

The publisher acknowledges the support of the Canada Council and the
Cultural Services Branch of the Government of British Columbia in making
this publication possible. We acknowledge the financial support of the
Government of Canada through the Book Publishing Industry Development
Program for our publishing activities.

For more information on other Whitecap Books titles,
please visit our web site at www.whitecap.ca

To Elizabeth Hutton
because every girl needs a mentor

Contents

Introduction

As soon as the sky is completely dark, the spy begins crawling towards enemy lines. Guards hold their rifles ready, searching for movement. If they spot her, they'll shoot on sight. But she keeps creeping forward. In her pocket, she has a tiny notebook and pen, ready to record the details of the enemy fort.

Does this sound like the beginning of an adventure novel? Not quite — it's the beginning of an adventure life! Disguised as a man, Emma Edmonds worked as an army nurse, then completed twelve spy missions.

The girls in *Canadian Girls Who Rocked the World* include a skier and a doctor, a journalist, a pop star, and a judge. They came from all parts of the country and spent their lives pursuing very different dreams. They had only one thing in common — they loved adventure. When a new discovery or a new chance beckoned, they were ready.

We've all heard of Joan of Arc, the French girl whose religious visions inspired her to lead an army. Like her, some of the girls in this book seemed born to greatness. Amazing things happened to them wherever they went.

But that's not the case for most of these girls. Most had to fight to achieve their dreams. Evelyn Hart was rejected twice by the National Ballet School — and she became one of the world's most famous dancers. Emily

Jennings Stowe was forced to operate her medical clinic illegally for thirteen years, but she refused to let discrimination win.

Every day, Canadian girls find new ways to rock the world. Some campaign for the environment, some organize new volunteer groups, and some pioneer business on the Web. Their secret? They're not content with "what I'm going to be when I grow up." They've got big ideas, and they're ready to rock the world right now.

Are you?

HOW TO ROCK THE WORLD
1 Choose your goal. Write it down as clearly as you can, so you can explain it to others.
2 Decide on the first step. Big goals have to be achieved bit by bit.
3 Enlist help. Most girls who rock have family and friends willing to lend a hand or offer advice.
4 Never give up! The girls in this book held on to their dreams through unbelievable challenges.

GIRLS WHO ROCKED THE SPORTS WORLD GIRLS WHO ROCKED THE GIRLS WHO ROCKED THE SPORTS WORLD GIRLS WHO ROCKED THE

Serious Sweat

Manon Rheaume

HOCKEY PLAYER
(1972 -)

anon heard the buzz of the crowd as she followed the rest of the Tampa Bay Lightning team down the long hallway to the ice. At 168 centimetres (five feet, six inches) tall and 61 kilograms (135 pounds), she was tiny compared to the other players. But Manon was used to that — she scarcely noticed the size difference any more.

The cheers grew louder. The announcer's voice boomed over the loud speakers and television cameras zoomed in on the hockey players.

"Breathe," Manon reminded herself.

She took her position in goal. The puck was dropped. It seemed as if the game were moving at double speed. Across the ice. Across again. Players passed the puck quickly back and forth until suddenly someone careened towards the net. He shot!

Slap! The puck bounced off Manon's padding. She'd made the save, but there was no time to stop and rest. One after another, players took eight more shots on goal. Pucks careened towards her at 160 kilometres an hour. Manon stopped all but two. At the end of the period, the game was tied 2–2, and Manon had become the first woman ever to play in the NHL.

Ever since she had been a toddler in Lac Beauport, Quebec, Manon had dreamed of playing for the National Hockey League. She began skating when she was three. Her brothers — one older and one younger — were both on a local hockey team, so Manon played goalie while they practised. They spent hours testing their skills in the basement and the backyard.

But Manon got tired of watching her brothers' games from the stands. When she was five, she asked to be the team goalie. When she skated onto the ice for her first game, she looked just like a boy — except for her white figure skates.

By the time she was eleven, Manon's team was the only one in the region to qualify for the Quebec International Pee Wee Hockey Tournament — a competition that had hosted such stars as Wayne Gretzky and Guy Lafleur. Manon was the first girl ever to play in the tournament. The year after, she became the first girl ever to play at the Bantam AA level.

Manon was one of the best goalies in the province. But not everyone thought a girl should play hockey. One coach said, "There's no way a girl is going to play on my team." Hockey was an obsession in Manon's hometown — with parents as well as players. And some of the parents felt that teaching a girl was a waste of time. After all, why train her when she would never make the NHL? When the Bantam AA players were invited to a summer training camp, Manon was excluded.

Discouraged, Manon quit playing hockey the week she turned seventeen. She began attending college near Quebec City. She had always been a good student, and she tried putting all of her energy into her studies. But she missed her time on the ice and the thrill of competition.

A year later, she discovered a women's team playing in Sherbrooke. It would be a two-and-a-half-hour drive to practice every week and practices were at nine or ten o'clock at night. As a women's team, it was hard to get ice time. Manon agreed to play anyway. The team trained hard and in 1991 they won the provincial championships and came in second in the nationals.

Her confidence back, Manon tried out for a new men's team starting in Louiseville. She competed against five other goalies for a spot on the team — and won. Before long, she was the first woman to goaltend in the Quebec Major Junior Hockey League.

FAST FACT

Manon married a roller hockey star, and the couple live in Las Vegas with their young son.

A year later, she was chosen to join the women's national hockey team on a trip to an international tournament in Finland. For weeks, the team trained for hours each day. They won all of their preliminary games. So did the American women's team. The Canadians won all of their games in the semi-finals. So did the Americans. The two teams met in the finals, both vying for the gold medal. The final score? Eight goals for the Canadians. Zero for the American team.

Soon after that, the Tampa Bay Lightning invited Manon to their training camp. On September 23, 1992, she played in the NHL exhibition game against the St. Louis Blues. She was twenty years old. When the media interviews and the phone calls and the autographs were over, Manon was a star!

Since her history-making game, Manon has played at national and world championships. At twenty-five, she travelled to Japan as part of Canada's 1998 Olympic Team and brought home a silver medal. She later turned

HOW WILL YOU ROCK THE WORLD?
I would like to play hockey in the World Hockey Championships, because I feel that I'm a pretty good hockey player and I enjoy playing hockey with other girls.

Zahra, age 10

her talents to professional roller hockey in Las Vegas, Nevada. Today, Manon helps a major manufacturing company design hockey gear especially for women.

FOR MORE INFORMATION
www.manonrheaume.com

Chelsea, age 13

HOW WILL YOU ROCK THE WORLD?
I want to be a famous athlete — a famous soccer player, and play on a professional soccer team. Also, I would like to be a famous volleyball player.

Nancy Greene

SKIER
(1943 –)

In 1958, the Canadian Junior Skiing Championships were held in the tiny town of Rossland, B.C. It seemed as if all 4500 residents of the town were involved, setting up the courses, advertising events, and scheduling races. One of the volunteers was fourteen-year-old Nancy Greene. Her older sister was racing, but although Nancy loved to ski, she'd entered few competitions. Instead, she was serving on the billeting committee, matching young skiers with host families for the event.

Then, the night before the races, the coach of the B.C. team called Nancy's home. Two members of the team had been injured on the slopes. Would Nancy race?

The next morning, she was standing at the starting gate, watching the girls before her struggle to complete the icy route. But there wasn't much time to get nervous. In just a few minutes, she was on her way down the slalom course, tucking to gain speed and slicing her skis hard to angle between the gates.

Some girls seem born for world-class competition. Swiss tennis star Martina Hingis held her first racket at age two. By the time she was fourteen, she was the top junior tennis player in the world.

Each skier races twice in the slalom event, and as Nancy headed up the lift for her second try, she heard the announcers call her time from the first run. Nancy was surprised. She thought she'd skied well, but the time was quite slow. Thinking her chances of winning were over, she completed her second run, and waited glumly at the bottom for the results.

She was third! The announcer had called the wrong time for Nancy's first run, and she soon found herself on the awards' platform. Along with her slalom award, she won second place in the downhill competition. Her older sister Elizabeth took first place in both races.

The 1958 championships sparked Nancy's taste for competition, and she trained hard the next year. In 1959, the event was held in Ontario, and she skied her best. Although a dislocated shoulder cut her competition short, her performance earned her an invitation to the training camp for the 1960 Olympics. After that, she competed in a series of U.S. races. Her hard work paid off, and she earned a spot on Canada's Olympic team.

Although her performance in the Olympics wasn't her best, this was to be the first of three Olympics and countless international competitions for Nancy. With each week on the slopes, her skiing improved.

In 1961, she and another skier from Rossland dreamed of racing in the season's European competitions. There, they would compete against the top skiers in the world again and again, constantly honing their skills. But at that time, there was no government support for amateur athletes. If Nancy wanted to go, she would have to pay her own way. Unfortunately, neither Nancy nor her family had the money.

Rossland to the rescue! Bursting with pride in their hometown skiers, the community began fundraising. In only two weeks, residents donated $3500 — enough for the two skiers to make the trip.

Over the next six years, Nancy entered countless competitions, sometimes winning, sometimes losing, and sometimes facing serious injuries. Her aggressive style led to some major tumbles, and Nancy dubbed herself "the queen of falls." And she wasn't only active on the slopes. Along with other Canadian skiers, she fought to change the way amateur athletics was funded. Nancy believed that the country's best athletes should be able to compete internationally, not just those with enough money to pay their own way. This was an issue she would continue to raise throughout her career.

In 1967, Nancy's years of practice came together. At the World Cup in Jackson Hole, Wyoming — the last World Cup of the season — she had to place first in three races to win. She won the giant slalom on Friday. She won it again on Saturday. Then came the hardest race — Sunday's slalom event. She was to ski against French champion Marielle Goitschel, a tough competitor. She could barely sleep the night before.

She won the race by seven-hundredths of a second. Nancy had won the World Cup, one of skiing's highest honours!

In 1968, Nancy stood on the podium in Grenoble, France, winner of an Olympic gold medal in the giant slalom and a silver in the slalom. Another World Cup and countless other competitions were hers by the end of the year. She skied one race so quickly, and won by such a large margin, that the timing equipment broke! Nancy earned international fame and proved that a small-town girl from B.C. could compete — and win! — against the best in the world.

FAST FACT

Nancy Greene was one of the first female athletes to lift weights as part of her training routine — the extra strength made her a more powerful skier.

When she gave up competitive skiing in 1968, she was offered product endorsement deals, she wrote her autobiography and a skiing handbook, and she served on a government task force to improve sport funding and management. In 1969, she married ski coach Al Raine.

Most recently, Nancy has been involved in the development of British Columbia ski resorts — first Blackcomb at Whistler, and now Sun Peaks.

There, visitors often see a sign that reads "Nancy is skiing today." Occasionally, someone gets a surprise lesson on the slopes.

FOR MORE INFORMATION

www.sikids.com/shorter/locker/canada/greatest/greene.html

www.nlc-bnc.ca/digiproj/women/women00/greene-e.htm

Jennie, age 11

HOW WILL YOU ROCK THE WORLD?

Before I am thirty, I would like to go to the Olympics for synchronized swimming. This has been my goal for a long time.

Barbara Ann Scott

**FIGURE SKATER
(1928 –)**

Barbara Ann was given her first pair of skates when she was six years old. A pair of brand-new, gleaming white figure skates was all she had been dreaming about for months. But when the gift finally arrived, she was in bed with an ear infection! Disappointed but not defeated, she laced on her skates and wore them in bed, the covers pulled aside so she could admire her feet.

When she recovered, Barbara Ann was allowed to take skating lessons on the condition that she also practise the piano every morning. By the time she was ten, she had completed the highest level of lessons at her local Ottawa skating rink. She entered her first competition that year — the Canadian Junior Ladies' Figure Skating Championship — and placed fifth. One year later, at only eleven years old, she won first place.

When they saw how serious Barbara Ann was about skating, her parents agreed to a new schedule. As long as she kept her grades high, Barbara would be allowed to miss her regular school classes, and study instead with a tutor in the afternoons.

In 1941, when she was twelve, she entered the Canadian Senior Ladies' Championship and placed second. Her performance earned her an invitation to the North American Championships in Philadelphia — the first of many international competitions.

By 1947, at nineteen, Barbara Ann was competing in the European Ladies' Championships in Switzerland and the World Championships in Sweden. She won both.

The next year, the young star — already famous in Canada and around the world — again entered the European Championships. In the 1940s, there were no indoor ice rinks. A week of bad weather had turned the rink at this competition to a pool of slush. Already battling the poor ice, Barbara Ann was flustered when her music stopped shortly into her program. Nonetheless, she won the competition.

GIRLS AROUND THE WORLD

One of Barbara's role models was French skater Sonja Henie. Sonja first competed in the Olympics at age eleven. In 1927, at fourteen, she became the youngest world champion ever.

In 1948, it was on to the Olympic Games in St. Moritz, Switzerland. There had been only two previous Olympic women's skating champions in history. The sport was relatively new, and many events had been cancelled during World War II. At this competition, twenty-five women would strive to become the world's third figure skating star.

Barbara Ann travelled to St. Moritz early to train in the high altitude. She practised for hours every morning. Some mornings she arrived at the rink so early that she helped the workers clear the night's snowfall off the ice.

On the day of the competition, two hockey games had already been played on the rink. The ice was rutted and rough. The woman before Barbara Ann fell three times. As she came off the ice, she generously showed Barbara Ann where the worst patches were. The skater quickly adapted her program to avoid them.

In the stands, her mother held her breath. Could her daughter complete her jumps without falling? She did! As the scores were announced and Barbara Ann became the first Canadian woman to win a gold at the Winter Olympics, the Canadian hockey team surrounded her and lifted her to their shoulders. The press dubbed her "Canada's Sweetheart," and Princess Elizabeth asked to meet her.

Barbara Ann was named Canada's Outstanding Female Athlete for three years in a row. She was inducted into Canada's Olympic Hall of Fame, Sports Hall of Fame, and Figure Skating Hall of Fame. She was also awarded the Order of Canada.

When she made her professional debut in December 1948, at the Roxy Theater in New York, Barbara Ann set up the St. Lawrence Foundation to distribute her earnings. The foundation paid the skater a salary and used the rest of her earnings — including about $80 000 for her appearance at the Roxy — to help underprivileged people and children with disabilities.

FOR MORE INFORMATION
www.nlc-bnc.ca/digiproj/women/women00/scott-e.htm

Moire, age 7

HOW WILL YOU ROCK THE WORLD?
I would rock Canada by becoming a famous skater, because I have been skating since I was two. I have done excellent triple axels and split jumps.

Abby Hoffman

RUNNER
(1947 -)

Abby took her place on the starting blocks, focussing all her attention on the 880-yard race ahead of her. The tall, lean nineteen-year-old had spent the last four years training for the 1966 Commonwealth Games in Jamaica, and now the final race of the games had arrived.

The starting gun cracked and the competitors leapt out of the blocks. The first lap was over in moments. Abby had stayed with the pack, slightly behind the race leaders. She was running fast — even faster than usual — but she knew she could finish the race.

Only half a lap to go. With a burst of determination, Abby picked up speed. She passed two runners easily. One more ahead of her. Another burst of speed. Side by side, Abby and Marise Chamberlain ran the final few strides. Could Abby win? She put all her training to work, her legs churning towards the finish line. And the gold medal was hers!

Abby won the race with a time of 2 minutes and 4.3 seconds — four seconds faster than she had ever run before. She was ranked among the six best 880-yard runners in the world.

Born in Toronto on February 11, 1947, Abby had always loved sports. The young tomboy refused to wear dresses and was never left out of her two brothers' high-energy games. In elementary school, she spent hours poring over her mother's scrapbook of female athletes — basketball players, tennis players, and track stars from the decades before.

In 1956, Abby decided to join the local hockey team. Although her parents thought the team would only accept boys, they agreed to take their daughter to the tryouts. Imagine their surprise when the coach called to say their son Ab had made the team. Their son?

It seems the coach had assumed Abby was a boy. The family decided not to tell, and Abby — or "Ab" — was one of the season's top players. When an official at an all-star game discovered the truth, the eight-year-old player appeared in newspapers and magazines across Canada and the United States.

Two years later, swimming caught Abby's attention. Rising at 6:30 a.m. to practise and returning to the pool every day after school, she steadily improved. She qualified for the Canadian championships in 1961.

But as Abby grew taller and thinner, other swimmers with short, muscular bodies surpassed her. Despite her determination and her rigorous training, she was no longer progressing as quickly. Abby's coach suggested she try track. There, her long, lean body might work to her advantage.

Abby took his advice, and joined the Toronto Olympic Club the same year. A few months later, she won her first big race, finishing an 880-yard run in Kitchener, Ontario, in only 2 minutes and 38 seconds. Within a year, she had won so many races that she was invited to try out for the Canadian track team, bound for the upcoming Commonwealth Games in Perth, Australia.

Fifteen years old, Abby met the top competitors in Canada at East York Stadium. And she won! But her high spirits were short-lived. When she competed in Perth, she discovered that Canadian runners were far behind their international counterparts. Without the coaching or training of the other runners, she finished last in the Australian event.

While the experience might have discouraged some athletes, Abby returned to Canada determined to improve. She began training up to twelve times a week. She woke early each morning to jog, she scheduled long-distance runs on weekends, and she spent each evening practising sprints and interval training with other runners.

Slowly, the high-school student began entering international races again. One of her first was a January 1963 competition in Boston. The crowd gasped as Abby tripped and fell near the beginning of the race. In an instant, she was 40 yards behind the other runners. Immediately, she scrambled to her feet. She set her eyes on the lead runner, and she shot past the other racers to the finish line. Her time of 2:17.5 tied the women's world record.

Two weeks later, she beat that record at a race in Winnipeg, setting her on the path to the 1966 Commonwealth Games in Jamaica, where, at nineteen, she won the gold medal.

FAST FACT

There were no women in the 1896 Olympics in Athens. But 100 years later in Atlanta, Georgia, almost 4000 women competed.

The rest of Abby's racing career reads like a whirlwind tour of the globe: Mexico in 1968, Germany in 1972, and Montreal in 1976. In Germany, she and six other female runners all broke the previous Olympic record in the 800-metre race.

As she gained fame in the racing world, Abby became a spokesperson for amateur athletes and helped form the Canadian Olympic Association. She raised money through donations and sponsorship, and helped to distribute funds for athletes' travel, training, and equipment costs. Her work led to countless new opportunities for girls in sport, and Abby was awarded the

Order of Canada — one of the highest honours the government can give to a Canadian citizen — in 1982.

FOR MORE INFORMATION
www.nlc-bnc.ca/digiproj/women/women00/hoffman-e.htm

Elizabeth, age 10

HOW WILL YOU ROCK THE WORLD?
I would like to go to the Olympics and win the gold medal for Canada in track and field 800-metre. I enjoy the 800-metre because I like to sprint at the end.

Evelyn Hart

DANCER
(1956 –)

When Evelyn stepped into the National Ballet School in 1967, she was eleven years old. She had never taken a dance lesson. She didn't even own a leotard. But when she heard that the prestigious ballet school was holding auditions, she begged her parents for the chance to attend. Ever since she had seen her first ballet on TV, she had dreamed of becoming a dancer.

Evelyn eyed the other girls nervously. Every one of them had a proper leotard and slippers. And as instructors led them through the audition, it was obvious that everyone else had taken lessons before. None of the instructors paid attention to Evelyn, struggling with new steps and positions. She had studied ballet books for months, but it wasn't enough.

When the letter from the National Ballet School arrived at her Ontario home, it said that Evelyn didn't have a dancer's body. She was crushed. But not for long! She pestered her mother for lessons, and two years later, this time with more confidence and experience, she auditioned again. Again, she was rejected.

One of the world's most famous dancers, Russian ballerina Anna Pavlova, fell in love with ballet when she was eight and gave her first public performance at eighteen. She continued dancing until her death in 1931, at the age of fifty.

Evelyn was not easily discouraged. In 1970, after her family moved to a town near London, Ontario, she began training with Dorothy and Victoria Carter. She convinced her father to install a barre in her bedroom and she spent hours stretching and practising. She completed two years of lessons in a single year, and in 1971, when she was fifteen, she auditioned a third time for the National Ballet School.

This time, she was accepted — with a full scholarship! But the intense pressure Evelyn placed on herself and the demands of the school proved too much. In December, her weight had dropped to thirty-four kilograms (seventy-six pounds). She was forced to leave the school and return home. The following fall, she found her place had been given to someone else.

A counsellor encouraged Evelyn to develop other interests, to give up the idea of becoming a dancer. But she wasn't ready to give up.

In 1972, she travelled to New York for summer workshops. There, she won the attention of her instructors and an invitation to train in New York once she finished high school. Finally, Evelyn's confidence grew.

In 1973, at age seventeen, she auditioned for the Royal Winnipeg Ballet's school, where instructors dubbed her "the wild one." They accepted her immediately. Within three years, she finished her training and entered the Royal Winnipeg Ballet. Soon she was dancing major roles in such ballets as the *Nutcracker* and *Sleeping Beauty*. By 1979, she was a principal dancer.

But Evelyn's crowning achievements came in 1980. First, she won

FAST FACT

The first ballet Evelyn ever watched was *Romeo and Juliet*. She saw it on CBC TV, performed by the National Ballet of Canada.

a bronze medal at the World Ballet Concours in Japan. Then, she travelled to Varna, Bulgaria, to compete in the dance world's most famous arena — the Varna International Ballet Competition. For sixteen days, she danced in front of countless judges and audiences. It was soon clear that the audiences loved her. But would the judges?

They did! She won the gold medal and, even more exciting, an Exceptional Artistic Achievement Award. Within days, newspapers were calling Evelyn the best young dancer in the world. Invitations poured in from around the world. Could Evelyn dance in Paris? In New Orleans?

Today, Evelyn has toured North America, Europe, and Asia. The Canadian government has awarded her the Order of Canada. And the young girl who dreamed of becoming a professional dancer is a Resident Guest Artist with the Royal Winnipeg Ballet.

FOR MORE INFORMATION

www.rwb.org

www.galadesetoiles.com/bios/hart.html

HOW WILL YOU ROCK THE WORLD?

I want to be a soccer player and get a degree in physical education, or I'd like to become a famous dancer. I feel nervous and excited when I race or play a big game in soccer.

Kristie, age 10

Marilyn Bell

SWIMMER
(1937 -)

I t was just after 11 p.m. when sixteen-year-old Marilyn slipped into Lake Ontario. The water was dark and cold, lit only by the glow of lights from Youngstown, New York. From the beginning, Marilyn set a determined pace. Fifty-five times a minute, her arms churned through the water. Her goal, a breakwater off Toronto, was more than fifty kilometres away.

There were two other women in Lake Ontario on the night of September 8, 1954. One was Florence Chadwick, an American marathon swimmer already famous for crossing the English Channel. The officials from the Canadian National Exhibition (CNE) had invited Florence to swim the lake, thinking her appearance would draw crowds and media attention.

The third swimmer was twenty-eight-year-old Winnie Leuszler. Like Marilyn, Winnie was an unofficial entry. The CNE officials had not planned for this event to be a race and although they allowed the two women to swim, they promised no special favours or prize money.

None of this mattered to Marilyn. Through the early hours of the morning, her stroke remained strong. When she passed the American star, she slowed her pace slightly to fifty strokes a minute. But all night, she never stopped to rest.

Winnie was pulled from the water after only a few hours. In the early morning, Florence quit, too ill to continue. Marilyn kept swimming. Her coach, following alongside in a motorboat, wrote encouraging messages on a blackboard, and held them over the water for her to read as she rose for breath.

During the day, a thirty-kilometre-an-hour wind whipped the water into choppy waves and blew Marilyn off course, making her path to the opposite shore even longer.

In Ontario, radio stations had picked up the story and news of Marilyn's attempt was soon broadcast across the country. By evening, crowds began to gather at the exhibition lakeshore. Vacationers extended their stays to watch for the swimmer to arrive. Marilyn's schoolmates crowded the shore. Bright pink flares shot into the air to help keep her on course as darkness fell. She had been swimming for one whole night and one whole day.

For a moment, Marilyn stopped. She floated in the water and turned exhausted eyes towards the boat. Her coach waited, allowing her to make her own decision. Her parents, in a boat just behind her, struggled to stay silent. Then, she turned back to the water and began her steady front crawl once more.

GIRLS AROUND THE WORLD

Girls continue to amaze the sports world. In 1987, at fifteen, American soccer star Mia Hamm was the youngest woman ever to play on the national women's team. In 1999, she led her team to first place in the World Cup.

Twenty hours and fifty-seven minutes after she began, Marilyn reached Canadian shores. To the cheers of thousands, she was lifted from the water and carried to a waiting ambulance. She was the first woman in history to swim Lake Ontario.

For those who heard the story on the news that day, Marilyn Bell was a new name. But swimming was nothing new to this athlete. Born in Toronto,

Marilyn took her first lessons at age nine, and entered her first mile-long swimming race only a year later. Used to swimming in a heated pool, not the frigid lake waters, she finished ninth in that race, and left determined to improve.

Marilyn joined the Lakeshore Swimming Club and began a rigorous training schedule, swimming from the Credit River to Lake Ontario and back again. When she was eleven, she finished the CNE's mile-long race in sixth place. At twelve, she finished second, only a split second behind the leader.

When she turned thirteen, Marilyn entered both the junior and senior mile-long races. But bad weather plagued the event, and the races were rescheduled — both to the same day. The senior women's race was first. Striving for the lead, Marilyn poured her strength and skill into the contest, and finished a close second behind a much more experienced swimmer. Then, just as she was drying off, the start of the junior race was announced. It was back into the water, and this time, the first-place ribbon was Marilyn's.

She was soon entering professional races and her swimming times continued to improve. But in 1954, she was disappointed to discover there would be no women's swimming races at the CNE that year. Not to be stopped, Marilyn asked her coach if she could join a teammate, Cliff Lumsden, as he competed in an Atlantic City race that July.

Atlantic City's Centennial Marathon was a twenty-six-mile route around Absecon Island in cold waters with challenging tides. After Cliff previewed the course, the pair spent days training in the most weedy, difficult sections of the Credit River. They then travelled to Atlantic City and spent more days battling the tides and racing against each other in practice drills.

A third Canadian, Tom Park, also decided to join the race. When the athletes set off, Tom and Cliff were almost immediately in the lead and they finished the race only moments apart, but well ahead of the American contenders.

Not long after the crowd had finished cheering for the men's achievements, they began cheering for Marilyn. She had outdistanced all the other women to claim first prize — $1150!

Just a few months later, she conquered the width of Lake Ontario and Marilyn Bell was suddenly a household name.

Before she retired from marathon swimming, she crossed the Strait of Juan de Fuca in British Columbia and, at seventeen, became the youngest person ever to swim the English Channel. Her achievements changed the world's ideas about women's athletic abilities and endurance.

FOR MORE INFORMATION

www.nlc-bnc.ca/digiproj/women/women00/bell-e.htm

Jennifer, age 11

HOW WILL YOU ROCK THE WORLD?
I would like to make an Olympic record in the 200-metre backstroke, because this would show that girls really rock Canada!

Frontier Femmes

GIRLS WHO ROCKED THE NEW WORLD GIRLS WHO ROCKED THE GIRLS WHO ROCKED THE NEW WORLD GIRLS

Victoria Belcourt Callihoo

TEAMSTER, FARMER, AND HISTORIAN
(1861-1966)

Thirteen-year-old Victoria held her breath as the Métis hunters rode fearlessly into the stampeding bison herd. With a shot, one of the massive animals fell. Another shot, another bison went down. More than a hundred men rode in the hunt. Most chose their targets and shot once before the herd passed them. Some of the best shot two or three times. Occasionally, an unlucky hunter was trapped in the roiling herd, his bones broken in the crush of frightened animals.

When that happened, Victoria's mother rushed to help. She was a medicine woman, and she followed the hunters well prepared with herbs and bandages.

Victoria's job began the next day. When the meat and hides had been stretched in the sun to dry, she fed small fires, giving the meat a smoky flavour and keeping the flies away.

Victoria had been born on November 19, 1861, in Lac Ste. Anne, a Métis community in Alberta. The Métis were the sons and daughters of native women and European fur traders and explorers. Belonging neither to the white community in Canada nor to the native groups, the Métis developed a strong culture of their own.

At seventeen, Victoria married a Métis man named Louis Callihoo. Together, the couple had six daughters and six sons. They farmed, they hunted, and they drove freight. In all of these things, Victoria was an equal partner. She once shot a bear at close range with her musket. She was an excellent teamster, driving her horses between Edmonton and Athabasca Landing, carrying Hudson's Bay Company supplies. And even after Louis's death in 1926, she continued to garden and farm in Lac Ste. Anne.

Living more than a century, Victoria saw many changes. Some, she didn't understand. Why try to accumulate money when you could trade furs for anything you might need? And some changes, she didn't seem to need. When she had her first doctor's appointment at age ninety-nine, the doctor told her she was in excellent health.

But some new developments, Victoria loved. At one hundred, she discovered she could talk to her children over the telephone — in Cree, Iroquois, or French.

In the 1950s, Victoria wrote about her vivid memories of Métis life. She told of the annual hunts, when families travelled farther and farther to find the disappearing buffalo. She wrote of the danger from the Blackfoot people, and the lifestyle of the Iroquois in Alberta. Her accounts

FAST FACT

Victoria loved to dance the Red River jig. She won a tanned buffalo hide for her performance in a dance contest when she was 74, and she danced the jig "the way it should be done" for her family at the age of 103.

were published in the *Alberta Historical Review* and they provided historians with one of the best views of traditional life on the prairies.

Victoria lived alone until she was 101. When she died, at 104, she had more than 240 children, grandchildren, great-grandchildren, and great-great-grandchildren living across the country.

Although Victoria never achieved fame or fortune, she lived at a time when life for Métis people was quickly changing. By adapting to that change and recording the ways of the past, she ensured that future girls would learn of her life and the life of her people. For her family and for women across the country, she was a symbol of strength and independence.

FOR MORE INFORMATION

www.nlc-bnc.ca/digiproj/women/ewomen1b.htm

HOW WILL YOU ROCK THE WORLD?
Right now I don't know what I want to be when I grow up, but I know I want to help kids in need and help out as much as I can.

Kym, age 12

Catherine O'Hare Schubert

PIONEER
(1835 – 1918)

Catherine lay quietly in bed. She could hear her older sister snoring softly beside her, but Catherine was wide awake. She thought about what she had packed, about the money set aside to buy her passage, about leaving her brothers and sisters. It was 1845 and she was setting sail for America early the next morning. She had already finished a course for domestic workers, or servants. Her plan was to arrive in New England and begin sending money home to her family as quickly as possible.

Catherine was one of tens of thousands of people who left Ireland in the late 1840s, escaping the starvation and poverty of the potato famine and hoping to find a new life. Catherine's father was a linen weaver, but as factories grew and provided cloth more cheaply than cottage workers could, he found it more and more difficult to feed his nine children. Anything Catherine could send home would help.

So the sixteen-year-old girl boarded a ship by herself. After a difficult and overcrowded passage and an impatiently spent time in quarantine to be certain she was healthy, Catherine found a job as a maid with a family in

Massachusetts. She worked hard and was soon able to send money home. In her spare time, she combed the family's library and taught herself to read.

In 1855, the year she turned twenty, Catherine married Augustus Schubert, a carpenter with a taste for adventure. The couple moved to St. Paul, where Augustus found work in the construction boom and Catherine opened a small grocery store, selling her own baking. The couple's first son, Gus, was born in 1856 and a daughter, Mary Jane, followed two years later.

Eventually, a drop in the demand for construction, tension with the native people of the area, and Augustus's restlessness led the family 900 kilometres north to Fort Garry (now the city of Winnipeg). They opened a small store and began farming. Catherine had a third child, Jimmy, in 1860.

Soon, talk of gold strikes in Saskatchewan began to filter through the town. Rumours about men earning instant riches sparked Augustus's imagination. Just as he was planning a trip to the province, a sternwheeler brought a group of about 150 men into town. They were the Overlanders, on their way to the gold fields of the Cariboo in British Columbia, which were said to be richer. The journey would be long and hard, but rewarding. Within a few days, Augustus was convinced. He announced that he was leaving Catherine to mind the store and the children. He was going to the Cariboo.

Not without me! That was Catherine's response. And when Augustus refused to take her, she left the house without telling him and went in search of Tom McMicking, a leader of the Overlanders. Tom told her that there were no other women on the trip, that it would be too dangerous, and that the trail was not a place for children. Catherine argued that being on the trail with her husband was no more dangerous than being left alone in the rough Fort Garry. Finally, Tom agreed.

GIRLS AROUND THE WORLD

Many women faced gruelling challenges to cross the continent. In the late 1700s, a sixteen-year-old Shoshone Indian, Sacagawea, acted as a guide for explorers Lewis and Clark on their route across the United States. She travelled with her newborn baby strapped on her back.

Of course, Catherine hadn't told him that she was four months pregnant.

When Augustus discovered what she had done, he was so angry that he threw their dishes against the wall. But Catherine had won the battle. On June 2, 1862, they started out on the trail with a cow, an ox, and a small wagon. Catherine rode a horse with five-year-old Gus and three-year-old Mary Jane in panniers on either side. Jimmy, not yet two, rode with his father.

From Fort Garry, they followed a winding route to Saskatchewan's Fort Carlton, then traced the banks of the Saskatchewan River towards Fort Edmonton. They fought mosquitoes and blackflies. They travelled through a blizzard, they were followed by wolves, and they trudged on through twenty days of continuous rain. A horse died from exhaustion. At one point, their native guide deserted them.

Despite these conditions, they managed the 1600 kilometres to Fort Edmonton by late July. There, they left the wagons and took only packhorses. Again, they faced formidable challenges. They waded through swamps and wiggled across cliff-top trails only thirty centimetres wide. Catherine made her children crawl on their stomachs, and held her breath until they were safe on the other side.

When they reached the Athabasca River, their food began to dwindle and they were forced to kill some of the animals. Men hunted along the way, but it was difficult to hunt and travel, and they were desperate to reach the Cariboo before winter.

Once in B.C., the group faced a difficult choice — take the Fraser River, which was faster but much more dangerous, or take the Thompson. Catherine, now eight months pregnant and eager to reach Kamloops as quickly as possible, voted for the Fraser. But the group overruled her, and they built rafts and dugouts to float down the Thompson.

Even the less dangerous route was filled with hidden hazards. One night, all of Augustus and Catherine's supplies were swept away in their dugout. Their companions generously pooled their resources to help the family. Still, well before they reached Kamloops, they were out of both food and ammunition. Catherine gathered rosehips along the riverbank — their only nutrients. And just when the situation seemed as if it couldn't get worse, Catherine went into labour on the raft.

Luckily, they spotted a Shuswap village on the banks and the women there helped deliver a healthy baby girl, named Rose for the rosehips that had sustained the family.

In October, they finally reached Kamloops. Catherine was the first European woman to arrive in B.C. by the overland route. At the time, the distinction didn't seem that important. She was much too busy farming and running an inn to support the family while Augustus panned for gold (unsuccessfully). She also began a small school for the local children.

Catherine had two more children after arriving in B.C. She served as the matron for the interior's first school, in Cache Creek, and she ran a number of successful inns in her new province. She died in 1918 at the age of eighty-three.

FOR MORE INFORMATION

www.bcarchives.gov.bc.ca/exhibits/timemach/galler10/frames/
schubert.html

Robin, age 13

HOW WILL YOU ROCK THE WORLD?
I want to be the first person to be frozen in time then "awaken" in the year 4017, bring future knowledge back (using time travel), and maybe cure some horrible diseases.

Madeleine de Verchères

SETTLER
(1678 – 1747)

Fourteen-year-old Madeleine Jarrett was working in the garden just outside her father's fort when she saw them. Iroquois warriors, masters of surprise, stepped suddenly from the woods. The men in the fields had no chance to escape, but Madeleine was closer to the fort than they were.

Sprinting towards the gate, she yelled, "To arms! To arms!" Just then, she felt a sharp yank as a warrior grabbed her scarf. She refused to stop. Instead, she ripped off the scarf as she ran, making the warrior stumble. She reached the fort seconds before him and slammed the gate.

But she wasn't safe yet. The two soldiers inside with the women and children had panicked. No one was thinking about defence, and the Iroquois were already fighting to get in. Again yelling "To arms!", Madeleine took charge. She grabbed a musket and ran from post to post, pretending there were many soldiers firing. When she spotted her younger brother, she ordered him to do the same. Soon, one of the soldiers appeared. Madeleine ordered him to take charge of the fort's cannon, firing as quickly as possible.

47

The combination of the cannon and the muskets convinced the Iroquois that the fort was heavily armed. They retreated. Still, Madeleine didn't relax. She watched the woods carefully for the rest of the day and throughout the night.

Madeleine wasn't usually left in charge of the fort. Her father's seigneury, a parcel of land granted to gentlemen or ex-soldiers in New France, was in a dangerous position. Fort Verchères was known as Fort Dangerous for its position along the Richelieu River, where Iroquois war parties would travel on their way to New France.

The fort had faced many attacks in the past and some settlers had been killed. But there were no attacks the summer of 1692. By fall, the settlers had relaxed. When Madeleine's father went to Quebec City on business and her mother went to Montreal for winter supplies, they were confident the fort would be safe under the eyes of two old soldiers.

But they were wrong. If not for Madeleine's quick thinking, all of the settlers might have been captured or killed. As it was, she worried that the Iroquois would reappear.

Fortunately, the cannon fire had alerted the surrounding forts. Soon, word was sent to Montreal and reinforcements were on the way. A hundred men headed downriver. Fifty more set off on foot. By the day after the attack, they reached the fort and went in pursuit of the retreating war party. When they found them, they discovered all but two of the captured farmers alive.

GIRLS AROUND THE WORLD

When the going gets tough, some women get their guns! Marina Raskova began flying at nineteen, and led the famous Russian Night Witches, a team of female fighter pilots, in World War II.

Madeleine's heroism earned her the nickname "Madeleine de Verchères, heroine of New France."

Perhaps her experience gave her an independent streak. Unlike most girls in New France, Madeleine didn't marry young. Instead, she ran the seigneury with her mother after her father's death in 1700. She was known as one of the colony's best shots with a musket and as a skilled duck and deer hunter. She eventually married a prosperous landowner in 1706, and the couple had five children.

Lauren, age 11

HOW WILL YOU ROCK THE WORLD?

I would like to invent a new machine that would take you anywhere you wanted, with just one touch of a button. This machine will save time and be convenient.

Sylvia Estes Stark

PIONEER
(1839 - 1944)

Sylvia heard banging and shouting outside the cabin. Quietly, she slipped out of bed and padded to the next room. The room was dark, but her mother and father were crouched beside the window. When her father saw her, he quickly pulled the eleven-year-old down beside him.

Outside, men with guns and torches surrounded the cabin. They yelled words like "nigger," and threatened to burn the house down. Sylvia had heard of these men before. People called them the "Klu-Kluks." The young girl stayed as still as she could and held her breath for what seemed like hours. Finally, the men went away.

Sylvia had been born a slave in Missouri in 1839. Her father, Howard, worked on a ranch owned by Tom Estes. Her mother, Hannah, worked in the house of banker Charles Leopold. Sometimes, her mother would tie a large apron around Sylvia's waist and, standing on a chair, Sylvia would carefully help dry the white family's dishes. Later, she took care of the Leopold children. By listening carefully while they did their homework, Sylvia was able to teach herself to read.

In 1849, Sylvia's father Howard was sent on a cattle drive to California, a state with no slavery. Tom Estes agreed that if Howard worked in the gold mines and sent back $1000, he could buy his freedom. It took months of work, but Howard eventually saved the money and sent it to Missouri. But Estes changed his mind! He kept the $1000 and refused to give Howard his freedom papers.

When Hannah's owner, Charles Leopold, heard the story, he offered to help. Howard saved another $1000 and sent it to Leopold. Leopold was able to buy the freedom papers from Estes and send them to California. Sylvia's father was finally a free man.

He continued to work in the mines, and by 1851 he was able to buy freedom for Sylvia, her brother, and her mother. The family bought a small farm in Missouri. But after white men surrounded the house, threatening to burn it down, they decided it was too dangerous to stay. The family travelled by horse and wagon across the country to Placerville, California, and bought a small farm. Sylvia was twelve years old.

At fifteen, she met and married an older dairy farmer named Louis Stark. Together, they raised cattle and began a small farm of their own. But California was growing more and more dangerous. Black people were not considered citizens, and could not testify against white people in court. That meant that if a white person claimed a black person's land, or harmed a black person, it was almost impossible to fight back.

When they heard about land available in British Columbia, Sylvia and Louis, along with Sylvia's parents, decided to move. They sold the farms and travelled north. Sylvia was only twenty-one, but she already had two children. By the time she and Louis claimed land on Salt Spring Island near Victoria, she was pregnant with a third. When she saw the small, roofless cabin that Louis had quickly built to shelter them, she was horrified.

The couple worked hard to build their farm. Within two years, the small cattle herd Louis had brought from California had doubled. But even on Salt Spring Island, the family was not safe from racism. Two labourers on the farm were shot, and Sylvia worried constantly about her children.

They moved twice more — first to a more populated place on Salt Spring Island, then, in 1875, to land near Nanaimo on Vancouver Island. But Sylvia was homesick, and soon moved back to Salt Spring Island with her son, Willis, leaving Louis to tend the Nanaimo farm.

A few years later, coal deposits were discovered beneath their Vancouver Island land. Coal was big business at the time, and powerful companies were interested in the rights. They offered to buy the farm from Louis and Sylvia, who refused. A short time later, Louis was found dead at the bottom of a cliff. He had been murdered, at age eighty-five. His sons believed that he was murdered for refusing to sell the land, but nothing could be proven.

FAST FACT

In the 1800s, slaves took the last names of their owners. Sylvia's last name was Estes because her father worked for Tom Estes. She later took her husband's last name, Stark.

Sylvia continued to farm on Salt Spring for more than forty years. She was respected as a knowledgeable farmer, an experienced midwife, and a kind and caring woman. Sylvia died at 106. Her children and grandchildren now live throughout Canada and the United States.

While still a child, this amazing woman had been forced to fight slavery, racism, and poverty. But she won her freedom and valued it until her death. Although few people have heard her story, Sylvia's life was special because of the huge obstacles she overcame to achieve a peaceful, happy home.

FOR MORE INFORMATION

www.bcarchives.gov.bc.ca/exhibits/timemach/galler10/frames/index.htm

Eunice Williams

MOHAWK   PIONEER
(1696 – 1785)

Screams and gunfire woke seven-year-old Eunice. She scooted from under the covers and crouched behind her bed while her older sister crept towards the window. Suddenly, the door to their room banged open. Two native men, their faces streaked with bright war colours, strode across the floor, scooped the girls up, and left the house. By the next morning, Eunice was marching north.

Mohawk warriors raided the New England town of Deerfield on February 29, 1704. They burned more than a dozen houses, killed men who tried to resist, and took 104 captives. The prisoners included Eunice, her father, her mother, and three of her brothers and sisters.

At the time, it was common for raiding parties to kidnap settlers. Queen Anne's War pitted France and allied native groups against the English. Kidnapping villagers helped terrify the enemy. Holding them for ransom helped bring in funds for ammunition. And the settlers who were killed or who chose to stay with the kidnappers weakened enemy numbers.

But seven-year-old Eunice knew little of this. She only knew that she was cold, hungry, and tired. Although her captors took pity on her and carried her much of the way, they never slowed their march. Captives who could not keep up were killed and scalped. Eunice's mother, weak from giving birth a few weeks before, was one of the unlucky.

Eunice's father was a strict Puritan minister. He saw their capture and the long march to a village near Montreal as punishment from God for his sins. When he was released after three years, he saw it as a sign of God's mercy. So he couldn't understand when his daughter refused to return to New England with him.

When she had arrived near Montreal, Eunice had been adopted by a Catholic native family who treated her as their own child. Having lost her mother, Eunice grew to love her new family and accept their faith. She lived with them for three years before her father was released. By that time, she didn't want to leave, and her adopted parents didn't want to let her go.

At sixteen, Eunice married a Mohawk man and the couple had three children — John, Catherine, and Sarah. To Eunice's father, her actions were a mystery. He couldn't believe she would want to stay, and he travelled north in 1714, the year after her marriage, to convince her to return to New England.

But Eunice had found happiness with the Mohawk people and no longer missed her first home. Eventually, she visited her brother,

GIRLS AROUND THE WORLD

Rigoberta Menchu was born in 1959 in a tiny Indian village in Guatemala, where her people faced starvation and constant persecution by the government. Rigoberta travelled among the villages, learning Spanish to communicate with different language groups, and taught her people how to protect themselves. Although members of her family were tortured and killed, she continued to work as an advocate for the Indian people. In 1992, she won a Nobel Peace Prize for her efforts.

FAST FACT

Eunice's new family renamed her Gannenstenhawi, "She brings in the corn."

54

a minister in a different New England settlement. But she returned to her Mohawk family and lived in New France until she died at the age of eighty-nine.

Ariana, age 12

HOW WILL YOU ROCK THE WORLD?

When I grow up I want to be a sports reporter and an interior designer. Also I want to be the manager/owner of a hotel in Beverly Hills.

Esther Brandeau

SHIP'S BOY
(CA. 1718 – UNKNOWN)

When Jacques La Fargue stepped off the ship in Quebec, the docks were packed with people. Labourers hustled cargo from the holds, port authorities conferred with the captain, and ladies gathered around the disembarking passengers, eager to see the latest fashions from France. In 1738, the colony of New France was firmly established, but news from Europe was always welcome.

There were so many people that some even found time to speak with the ship's boy, a youngster who barely looked old enough to shave. But when they spoke to Jacques, they found him more refined than they had expected. And they were flabbergasted when he revealed that he was not a ship's boy at all — he was a ship's girl!

The new arrival declared that she was Esther Brandeau, and that she was a Jew. That news threw the colony into a frenzy. New France held strictly to the Roman Catholic faith. No non-believers could be allowed to wander freely. But even so, the prison wasn't suitable for a girl. In desperation, the Intendant of the colony had her placed in the hospital, under guard. Priests, nuns, and community leaders were sent, with instructions to report back to the Intendant when the girl had converted to Catholicism.

There was just one problem. Esther refused to convert. And as she told her story, it became more and more apparent that she wouldn't be forced to do anything.

Esther claimed that her father was David Brandeau, a French merchant. When she was fifteen, she had boarded a Dutch ship, on her way to visit an aunt and brother in Amsterdam. But the ship had been wrecked off the coast of Bayonne and Esther had been taken in by a kindly Roman Catholic woman. Soon, she found herself eating pork — something forbidden to Jews.

Esther began to wonder what else was forbidden. What else were Christians allowed to do that Jews were not? In fact, now that she had disappeared from her family's sight, what was to stop her from doing anything she liked?

Two weeks after the shipwreck, she disguised herself as a boy and went to work on a trading ship. In the next few years, she served on several voyages, worked in a tailor's shop, and joined an infantry division. She never stayed long in one place and soon her curiosity led her to the *Saint-Michel*, a ship bound for New France.

Eventually, when Esther refused to convert, the Intendant of the colony appealed to the King of France, sending word of the situation by ship. Louis XV replied that the girl could not be tolerated in the colony. She was to be deported immediately.

After living in New France for about a year, Esther sailed back to France aboard the *Comte de Matignon,* her passage paid by the king. She may not have become an official Canadian, but she certainly gave it her best effort. Our history books now name her the first Jew to live in the country.

HOW WILL YOU ROCK THE WORLD?
I would like to be the first person or woman to go to Mars. I'd like to see what being in space is like and, because I want to work at NASA, I might have a good chance of doing it.

Alex, age 11

GIRLS WHO ROCKED THE ARTS WORLD GIRLS WHO ROCKED THE GIRLS WHO ROCKED THE ARTS WORLD GIRLS WHO ROCKED THE

In the Limelight

Alanis Morissette

SINGER
(1974 -)

Strobe lights flashed and Alanis bounded onto the stage, waving her signature peace sign at the audience and swinging her long, straight hair. Thousands of fans screamed their welcome and, as the star broke into one of her newest hits, the audience mouthed the words along with her.

This scene was repeated across Canada and around the world in 1995 as *Jagged Little Pill* broke record after record. Only months after its release, 16 million copies had been sold in the United States alone, placing it firmly on the list of the top twelve bestselling albums in history. Soon, it hit the 20 million mark. And while radio stations struggled to keep up with requests for such songs as "You Oughta Know" and "Hand in My Pocket," sales reached 28 million, making *Jagged Little Pill* the top-selling album in history by a female singer. Alanis was twenty-one years old.

Her rise to stardom began when she was still a toddler. Born in Ottawa on June 1, 1974, her parents took her to see the movie *Grease* when she was just three. Immediately, Alanis was fascinated. She had soon memorized the songs and was willing to entertain any audience, using a nail polish bottle as her microphone.

63

When Alanis visited Mother Teresa's hospital, she saw the work of another girl who changed the world! Mother Teresa became a nun and began teaching in Calcutta, India, at only eighteen. She later founded her own order, serving the needs of the poor and disabled in the slums of the city.

By the time she was nine, she was writing and singing her own songs. When she was cast in 1984 in the children's show *You Can't Do That on Television,* she saved her earnings and used them to create her own recording company and produce her first single, a song called "Fate Stay With Me." That single caught the attention of an agent, and Alanis spent the next few years singing wherever she could — sports events, rallies, and festivals. At fourteen, she shot her first music video.

Alanis's career took off when she was seventeen. In the era of heavy makeup, leather jackets, and big hair, she produced a self-titled album and was soon wowing pop audiences. When she released a second album, *Now Is the Time,* in 1992, she was awarded a Juno for Most Promising Female Vocalist of the Year.

But that promise didn't keep. As grunge took over from pop, Alanis disappeared from the music scene. The next few years were filled with rejections and challenges. In 1993, the nineteen-year-old moved to Los Angeles where, almost immediately, she was mugged at gunpoint. But instead of giving up on her music career, she channelled her anger into a series of harsh, emotional songs — the basis of *Jagged Little Pill.*

When the publicity and the tours were over, an exhausted Alanis retreated from the limelight. Believing she might never write songs again, she travelled to India for a six-week journey. There, she hiked the Himalayas, visited

FAST FACT

Did you know Alanis is a twin? Her brother Wade is a yoga instructor in Vancouver.

Mother Teresa's Missionaries of Charity Hospital, and rediscovered her love of music.

When she returned, Alanis and her co-writer Glen Ballard created the songs for her second album, *Supposed Former Infatuation Junkie,* in just three months. Although it didn't reach the highs of *Jagged Little Pill,* it certainly made an impression on the charts.

Today, Alanis has won four Grammy Awards, a Juno, and two MTV Video Awards. She has made a lasting impression on the North American music scene. Performers such as Fiona Apple have credited her with opening the door for female singers and songwriters. And thousands of fans impatiently await her next album.

FOR MORE INFORMATION
www.absolutedivas.com/alanis
www.alanismorissette.com/home.html

HOW WILL YOU ROCK THE WORLD?
I think all girls rock Canada! Ever since I was young I have always wanted to be a singer. Shania Twain is who inspired me.

Lindsay, age 13

Kathleen Parlow

VIOLIN VIRTUOSO
(1890 – 1963)

Five-year-old Kathleen walked the steep streets of San Francisco holding her mother's hand. The pair had just arrived and the bustling city was full of intriguing people and sights. Suddenly, something in a shop window caught Kathleen's eye. It was a tiny violin, perfectly made but half the size of a regular instrument. Kathleen loved small things, and she immediately pulled her mother to a stop. She had to have it.

As Kathleen kept pleading, her mother Minnie — who played the violin herself — gave way. If Kathleen would promise to take lessons, she could have the instrument. Kathleen promised. And took her first step towards becoming a violin virtuoso.

Kathleen was born in 1890 in Fort Calgary, Alberta, where her father worked for the Hudson's Bay Company. There, she learned words of the local Blackfoot people's language before she learned English. Her father loved the native traditions, and would spend long evenings sitting by the fire and telling legends to Kathleen.

But her father also loved whiskey and women. When Minnie discovered that her husband had a mistress, she took her daughter and ran away to San Francisco.

After Kathleen's first few violin lessons, Minnie took her to play for a cousin who was a music teacher. The cousin declared Kathleen a musical prodigy. "Nonsense," Minnie said. Relatives were always biased.

Today, another young musician is changing the way the world views the violin. Born in Singapore in 1978, Vanessa-Mae Nicholson played in her first concert at age ten. At thirteen, she began playing the electric fiddle, and now her audience includes both classical music and pop rock fans.

But Kathleen learned at an amazing rate. She gave her first concert at age six, and was soon playing to entertain family and friends. Through one small party, she met Mrs. Carolan, a society woman who arranged for Kathleen to study with the famous violinist Henry Holmes, once the teacher of Queen Alexandra.

Again, she learned quickly. When she was fourteen, Holmes suggested she study in England. Her church raised money for a new violin, and Mrs. Carolan supplied the tickets. Kathleen and Minnie were off to Europe.

The trip was difficult at first. One of Kathleen's concerts was postponed when she caught a bronchial infection. Their finances dwindled quickly. Then Minnie found a job with a women's club, Kathleen's performances began winning enthusiastic reviews, and Queen Alexandra invited the girl to play. Suddenly, the future seemed bright.

Kathleen was offered a chance to take her violin on a tour of North America, but she thought that was overly ambitious. She travelled to Russia to study in the conservatory of Leopold Auer — the first foreigner to study there.

By the time she turned eighteen, Kathleen had given concerts in Russia, Germany, Scandinavia, and London. During her first North American tour in 1910, she played in Montreal, New York, and Philadelphia. She travelled west to play a triumphant concert in her hometown of Calgary, then on to Vancouver and Victoria.

On her second North American tour, Kathleen met an inventor named Thomas Edison. He asked if he could record her music, and soon the sounds of her violin were travelling across the continent on phonograph records.

Kathleen never married. She once told an interviewer that she could only love another musician, and since she could never get along with other musicians, she probably shouldn't marry one.

Instead, she travelled the world, with her mother as her constant companion. In the early 1920s, she gave her first radio performance. In 1922, she toured Asia, and in 1925, she left Britain for good and moved to North America.

Unwilling to become a U.S. citizen, Kathleen settled in Toronto, where she accepted a teaching position at the Toronto Conservatory. There, she continued playing and teaching — even after a fall dislocated her shoulder. In 1963, at the age of seventy-three, she fell and broke her hip. She never recovered, and died of a heart attack a few months later, on August 19. Among music lovers, Kathleen is still celebrated as one of the greatest violinists in Canadian history.

FAST FACT

On one of her North American tours, Kathleen played in a benefit concert to raise money for the survivors of the *Titanic*.

FOR MORE INFORMATION

www.nlc-bnc.ca/digiproj/women/ewomen2d.htm

Lisa, age 14

HOW WILL YOU ROCK THE WORLD?

I want to do something that no man has ever done. Break a world record, invent a cure, or something like that. I want all men to say, "Wow, I wish I was a girl."

Emma Albani
(Lajeunesse)

DIVA
(1847 - 1930)

Each year the Convent of the Sacred Heart held an essay competition. The winner read her work at an end-of-term assembly. On the year Emma won, she practised reading her essay aloud again and again. She practised in front of the mirror. She read it to her father. She read it to the nuns so many times that she almost had it memorized. Finally, she felt confident enough to read it on stage.

On the day of the assembly, the seventy convent students filed into the room. The priests and nuns followed behind them. Even a few parents and townspeople stood at the back. It was time for the essay reading. But Emma had been nervous that day as soon as she woke up. She was even more nervous as she climbed the steps to the stage, and when she turned around to speak, her voice refused to come. She stood mute and terrified until one of the priests came to her rescue.

"Sit down, my child," he said. "You cannot recite, but I know if you had to sing it we should all hear it."*

* Emma Albani, *Forty Years of Song* (New York: Arno Press, 1977).

71

The priest was right. Emma had been singing since she was four. She had been born in 1847 in the small town of Chambly, near Montreal. Her mother, an amateur musician, began her training and her father, who played the organ, violin, harp, and piano, continued it. Before she began school, she was practising for four hours each day. By the time she turned eight, she could sight-read even complicated classical music.

Emma's mother died that same year. Because her father taught music classes there, Emma and her younger sister were able to enroll in the Convent of the Sacred Heart. Emma studied both her schoolwork and her music diligently, and when she was eight she sang in her first concert. But as she grew older, she was sometimes unsure about her future. Singers were not always viewed as they are today. In fact, some people thought women didn't belong on the stage. They thought of singers and actresses as little more than prostitutes. Life as a nun would be easier and more respectable.

Emma discussed her fears with the convent's Mother Superior. The nun told Emma that God had given her a beautiful voice, and she should consider it her duty to use it. In a few years, if her music career didn't work out, then she could consider life in the convent. That was all the encouragement Emma needed.

Her father was a restless man. When Emma was fourteen, he moved his family to Albany, New York. There, Emma was appointed first soprano at the Roman Catholic Church of St. Joseph. Her performances attracted more and more attention, and her sunny personality attracted well-wishers. When she was advised to study in Europe, the church held fundraising concerts to send her on her way.

So, at twenty-one, Emma arrived in Paris. Friends at home had given her a letter of introduction to Madame la Baronne de Lafitte, whose home was a gathering place for musicians of the day. Despite a bout of typhoid fever, Emma was soon studying with Gilbert-Louis Duprez, one of the city's most famous tenors. After six months under his tutelage, she travelled to Milan to study with Maestro Lamperti, a famous Italian instructor.

But Emma had limited funds for study. Many Italian opera companies were offering her roles, and she would soon have to accept one to support herself. With Maestro Lamperti's help, she chose to debut in *La Sonnambula* in Sicily. She was an instant success. In her first performance, she had fifteen curtain calls. In Italy at the time, sopranos were regarded like today's pop stars. News of her performance travelled quickly, and she was soon on her way to becoming a household name.

The name she was known by was "Emma Albani." One of her teachers had thought Lajeunesse was too difficult for Italian audiences. He suggested Albani, a traditional Italian name. Because of her time in Albany, New York, Emma happily agreed to the change.

Her debut in Sicily was soon followed by appearances in Florence, Malta, and London. In fact, London's Covent Garden became her base for seven years. In the off-seasons, she would travel to English music festivals or to performances in Paris or Russia.

In 1874, she made her first trip back to New York. Her agent on the American tour was Ernest Gye, the son of Covent Garden's manager. As the tour progressed, so did a romance, and Emma and Ernest were married soon after they returned to Britain. Emma's fame continued to grow, and she became known around the world.

FAST FACT

For a small-town Canadian girl, Emma Albani moved in high circles. During her career, she sang for the royalty of Britain, Holland, Russia, Italy, and Austria.

In 1883, she and Ernest again sailed to New York, en route to a Canadian concert tour. When they arrived by train in Montreal, the station was so full of cheering fans that the couple could barely get through. Emma was Canada's first celebrity, and as she travelled coast to coast, Canadian music lovers were determined to show their appreciation.

Emma sang in opera houses around the world for four decades. She sang forty-three roles, some of which were written specifically for her rich soprano voice. She was a personal friend of Queen Victoria, and admirers showered her with gifts and jewels.

In her seventies, however, Emma found herself living as a widow in Canada, no longer able to support herself by singing or teaching. People were shocked to discover that she'd had to sell her jewels. Fundraising efforts and benefit concerts, along with a pension from the British government, allowed her to live once more in relative comfort until her death in 1930.

FOR MORE INFORMATION
www.nlc-bnc.ca/women/ewomen2a.htm

Ashley, age 12

HOW WILL YOU ROCK THE WORLD?
When I get older I know that I will be a successful actress. I have wished for as long as I can remember that I would get a starring role and win a huge award for it.

Dorothy Livesay

POET
(1909 – 1996)

Dorothy was so excited that her classroom felt like a jail cell. She wiggled in her desk, and the piece of paper she held quivered. Unable to resist any longer, she passed it to a classmate, then to another.

"Dorothy!" The mathematics teacher's voice was sharp. Dorothy and her note were summoned to the front of the class.

But it wasn't a note — it was a cheque! *The Vancouver Province* had printed Dorothy's first poem, and her cheque for two dollars had arrived that day. At thirteen, she was officially a published poet.

Dorothy was born in Winnipeg on October 12, 1909. Her parents were both journalists. Their house was filled with books, magazines, and newspaper clippings.

So it was no surprise that soon after the family moved to Toronto in 1921, Dorothy began writing poetry. She carefully hid her efforts from her family, stashing her poems in the back of a dresser drawer.

Then, at thirteen, Dorothy came home from school to find her mother clutching a collection of poems, and excitedly reading one after another. Dorothy was furious. How could her mother read her private papers? But it was hard to stay angry when her mother was so enthusiastic. Eventually, Dorothy agreed to submit her work to publishers. After her first poem in the *Province,* her work appeared in more newspapers and magazines and she won several writing awards. With the help of her father and her best friend, Gina, she also published *Fortnightly Frolics of the Lower Fifth,* a magazine of character sketches and school gossip. The first two issues were received enthusiastically by the students, but when the principal found one he banned all future issues.

Dorothy began university and published her first chapbook of poetry, *Green Pitcher,* in 1928. She studied in France for a year, then returned to Toronto to earn an arts degree in modern languages in 1931, and published her second book, *Signpost,* in 1932. In 1934, she earned a diploma in social work.

Influenced by her father's liberal views and faced daily with extreme poverty in her life as a social worker, Dorothy was soon involved in social activism. She joined the Communist Party and the Progressive Arts Club and added her voice to public calls for social programs and government reform.

Despite winning two Governor General's Awards (for *Day and Night* and *Poems for People*), it was many years before Dorothy could earn a living solely as a writer. Between 1936 and 1963 she edited a magazine, taught high school, worked for the United Nations, and travelled to Africa to train teachers there. She married in 1937 and had two children.

FAST FACT

The government named Dorothy an Officer of the Order of Canada in 1987, one of the highest honours a Canadian citizen can receive.

Throughout everything else, she continued to write — poems, articles, and even radio plays.

After 1964, her work began to gain recognition around the world. She taught future writers at the University of British Columbia, the University of New Brunswick, the University of Alberta, and the University of Toronto. She published several books of poetry along with a collection of short stories, *A Winnipeg Childhood,* and a novel, *The Husband.* In 1991, she completed her memoirs, *Journey with My Selves.*

Dorothy began writing at a time when there were few female writers and almost no recognized Canadian writers — male or female. Her achievements paved the way for generations to come.

FOR MORE INFORMATION

www.harbour.sfu.ca/bcbook/people/livesay.html

HOW WILL YOU ROCK THE WORLD?

I want to have written a fantastic novel by the age of twenty-eight. I have been working towards my goal by competing in a writing competition, getting first prize, and writing my own story and performing it on TV.

Robin, age 10

Qiu Xia He

MUSICIAN
(1963 -)

Q iu Xia was dressed in her best clothes. She had been practising for weeks, and it was finally performance night. She wriggled impatiently as her mother fixed her hair. Then suddenly she was on stage, singing and dancing with other five-year-olds before a beaming group of parents and teachers.

Qiu Xia doesn't remember what she sang that night — it was the first of many performances. But she does remember hearing the applause and loving the feeling of being on stage.

Her mother and father loved music, and they were thrilled when their little girl showed talent. They enrolled her in a special elementary school in China. In the mornings, the students would work quickly to complete their regular schoolwork. Afternoons were devoted to dance and music; evenings were filled with rehearsals and performances.

Qiu Xia loved all kinds of music, but her favourite instrument became the pipa. Shaped like a long teardrop, the pipa is a four-stringed lute that looks a little like a guitar. It is made of polished wood with ox horn, jade, or bamboo frets, and it sounds unlike any other instrument in the world.

Soon, Qiu Xia's skills on the pipa were amazing her teachers. At only thirteen, she was asked to play in a professional music group. When she was nineteen, the prestigious Xian Academy of Music accepted her as a student and four years later she became an instructor there. As well as the pipa, she learned to play the gu gin, also called the Chinese zither.

In 1989, Qiu Xia's music brought her to Canada as part of a touring group. Although her family was still in China and all the other musicians from the group were returning, she decided she would stay in Vancouver. For a twenty-six-year-old who spoke almost no English, it was a brave decision.

In the next five years, Canada became the young virtuoso's adopted country and she dedicated herself to learning the language and establishing a career in a new land. She worked part-time jobs, performing on evenings and weekends until, finally, she began achieving recognition.

In her first few years in Vancouver, she met a few other Chinese musicians and together they formed a group named Silk Road. They played traditional instruments, introducing audiences in their new country to the sounds and compositions of China.

Shortly after, Qiu Xia started another group called Asza. Rather than specializing in one kind of music, Asza played songs from around the world, from Brazilian rhythms to Celtic folk. For Qiu Xia, it was a chance to use her traditional instruments in a dramatically different way.

FAST FACT

Look for Qiu Xia's name on the following CDs: *Village Tales, Endless, CBC — The Neighbourhood, The Spirit Emerges,* and *Asza.*

Today, both Silk Road and Asza have produced CDs and performed across North America, as well as in such places as Singapore and Thailand. And while Qiu Xia still plays many traditional pieces, her experiences have helped her develop a unique musical voice of her own. She now composes original music, combining the influences of China, Canada, and the world music she's been playing for the last few years. To her, that's the most exciting thing about being a musician — the chance to develop a new voice and new music that are completely her own.

FOR MORE INFORMATION
www.asza.com
www.festival.bc.ca/top30/silkroad.html

Tania, age 11

HOW WILL YOU ROCK THE WORLD?
During my lifetime I would like to be a very good musician and be recognized all across Canada as "The Best Pianist of the Century."

Emily Carr

ARTIST AND WRITER
(1871 – 1945)

Sixteen-year-old Emily stood outside the office of James Lawson, her legal guardian, and took a deep breath. Lawson was an important man in Victoria, with many wards; he wouldn't have much time for her. And she'd come without telling her older sister, Dede. If Emily was going to do this, she would only have one chance.

Determined, she stepped inside.

"Mr. Lawson," she said, "I would like to go to art school in San Francisco."

Lawson leaned back in his chair, not sure what to do. He knew that Emily and her sister, Dede, didn't always get along. He knew Emily had refused to return to school after her father's death. But to send her, alone, to art school in San Francisco?

Emily was honest with him. No, she said, she didn't get along with Dede. But this wasn't just a ploy to leave home. She'd been taking art lessons in Victoria for years, and she was sure. She wanted to be an artist.

Half impressed and half amused, Lawson agreed. If her sister could find her a place to stay, he would pay her way. And Emily's art career was born.

GIRLS AROUND THE WORLD

A school bus accident when she was eighteen left Frida Kahlo a permanent invalid. But to fill her time, the Mexican girl began painting — still lifes, landscapes, and, especially, self-portraits. By the time she died in 1959, her amazingly original work had earned her a spot among Mexico's most famous artists.

Richard Carr had brought his wife and two small daughters — Clara and Edith (Dede) — from England to Victoria in 1863. His importing business and his family boomed. Three more daughters arrived — Elizabeth (Lizzie) in 1867, Alice in 1869, and Emily in 1871. A son, Richard Henry, followed in 1875.

Emily spent her childhood singing in the family cowyard, making trouble for her older sisters, and walking her father to work each morning. But tragedy struck the year she turned twelve — her mother died of tuberculosis. Emily's father passed away two years later, leaving the younger children in the care of Dede (Clara had already married) and under the guardianship of Lawson.

Dede controlled the house with strict rules, and Emily soon rebelled. She refused to return to school the year after her father died, and when Dede wouldn't pay for art lessons, Emily traded lesson time for the use of her plaster casts. But she was restless. Two girls she studied with — Sophie Pemberton and Theresa Wylde — left to practise sketching and painting in Europe, and Emily hated to be left behind. She set her sights on the California School of Design. When she finally packed her bags in 1890, she couldn't have been more excited.

Emily spent five years in San Francisco, painting, scraping her canvas, and painting again according to the whims of her instructors. Although her hot temper remained with her — she once stormed out of a class after her instructor made her begin a work over — she made close friends and was thrilled to be out from under Dede's thumb.

At twenty-four, Emily returned to Victoria, converted the loft of the family's cow barn into a studio, and began teaching children's art classes. In the evenings, she would work on her own paintings and invite friends for small parties.

82

One summer, a missionary friend invited Emily and her sister Lizzie to Ucluelet. Lizzie could help teach at the mission school and Emily could sketch the native village. At first, Emily was shy and uncertain, asking tentatively if she could sketch people's houses. But she was welcomed by the Nuu-Chah-Nulth people, and soon she was wandering uninvited in and out of homes. The locals gave her the nickname Klee Wyck — the laughing one. Emily's experiences that summer sparked a lifetime interest in the West Coast forests, native people, and their history.

On the steamship back from Ucluelet, Emily met purser William "Mayo" Locke Paddon, a man who quickly fell in love with her. The son of an Anglican priest, Mayo lived in Victoria when not working on the ship, and he asked if he could visit Emily there.

But while she liked Mayo, Emily returned to Victoria and fell in love with someone else. Who? No one knows, but Emily's journals refer to a man she loved — a friend of her sisters — who left her life after a short time. She wrote nothing else about him, but we do know that she repeatedly turned down marriage proposals from Mayo.

Once again, Emily was teaching children's art classes. But she carefully saved her profits. By 1890, she'd hoarded enough money to study art in England. The next few decades brought more travel, more teaching in Vancouver, gallery exhibits, and work as a political cartoonist. Emily studied for a time in France, and took more journeys to sketch along B.C.'s West Coast. She developed a unique style, based on the "New Art" she studied in France. Broad, bold brush strokes and vibrant colours dominated her paintings.

However, despite the attention Emily's work brought in the newspapers and galleries, she was always stung by criticism. She called her paintings her children. She was

FAST FACT

To the society ladies of Victoria, Emily was a strange creature. She smoked, she refused to ride side-saddle (as proper ladies of the time did), and she owned a pet monkey named Woo.

pleased by positive reviews, but crushed by comments from people who didn't like her style, or preferred more conservative works.

When the Depression hit and paintings were no longer selling, Emily gave up her art, returned to Victoria, and opened a boarding house. She made pottery, raised sheepdogs, and didn't paint for fifteen years.

The most important events in Emily's career began to unfold when Eric Brown, curator of Canada's National Gallery in Ottawa, heard of her work through an anthropologist. He wrote to Emily and asked her to submit to an exhibition called Canadian West Coast Art, Native and Modern.

She was hesitant — after all, she hadn't painted in more than a decade — but she gathered her best works and travelled across the country. In Ottawa, she toured the studios of the Group of Seven, probably the most famous painters in Canadian history. She met one of the group's best known artists, Lawren Harris, and fell in love with his work. When Harris praised Emily's work in return, she was thrilled. Her inspiration returned, and she began painting again, more determined than ever.

Soon, Emily was one of the most famous artists in the country. Her paintings were selling so well that even her sisters — usually embarrassed by her nontraditional work — offered praise. For a few decades, Emily enjoyed the recognition that she had sought since moving to San Francisco in her teens.

At seventy, poor health forced Emily to end her trips up the West Coast. She could no longer paint, yet she longed for something creative to do. She decided to write. After an early rejection, her stories of travelling to small native villages were accepted for publication. *Klee Wyck* was released in 1941, and won a Governor General's Award.

HOW WILL YOU ROCK THE WORLD?
I would like to be an artist because I like to paint and sketch nature.

Lauren, age 6

More books soon followed: *The Book of Small,* about her childhood, in 1942; *The House of All Sorts,* about the boarding house days, in 1944; and *Growing Pains,* her autobiography. Emily died on March 2, 1945, shortly before *Growing Pains* was released.

FOR MORE INFORMATION
www.bcarchives.gov.bc.ca/exhibits/timemach/galler10/frames/carr.html
www.tbc.gov.bc.ca/culture/schoolnet/carr/

May Irwin

ACTOR AND SINGER
(1862 - 1938)

Beatrice Byke is a stunning young woman, pursued by many strange and unlikeable men. To escape them, she poses as the widow of Mr. Jones. Unfortunately, Mr. Jones is alive!

The part of the Widow Jones was May's first starring role on the vaudeville stage. She danced and pranced through her part, tricking and shocking the audience into laughter. Vaudeville was all about entertainment, and May was born to entertain. The stars of the vaudeville stage were as well known as Hollywood actresses are today.

May was born Georgina May Campbell in 1862 in Whitby, Ontario. Her father died in her early teens. Usually, young women supported themselves by teaching or sewing. Not May! She and her sister wanted something much more risqué — a career on the stage. They took the names May

FAST FACT

Even in old age, May had a flair for drama. At her request, she was buried in a vivid scarlet satin dress.

and Flo Irwin, and set out in search of fame.

The sisters made their debut in 1875 and acted at countless small clubs for about six years. After that, the pair went separate ways and May began to perform solo. In 1895, she finally got her big break. After she thrilled audiences with *The Widow Jones,* she was soon making up to $2500 a week. United States President Woodrow Wilson once invited her to perform, and thought she was so funny that he jokingly offered her a position as Secretary of Laughter.

In 1896, Thomas Edison invited May to Orange, New Jersey, to record a film version of *The Widow Jones.* The script called for a long kiss with co-star James C. Rich — the first kiss to be caught close-up on film.

May married her manager, Kurt Eisfeldt, in 1907. She had two sons, and retired from the stage in 1920. Her recordings, along with real estate profits, eventually made her a millionaire. She retired to property in Ontario's Thousand Islands and died in 1938.

FOR MORE INFORMATION

www2.nlc-bnc.ca/gramophone/src/irwin.htm

HOW WILL YOU ROCK THE WORLD?
All my life I've wanted to be an actress. Acting would be really fun for me because I like to talk, laugh, travel, and have fun.

Hilary, age 10

GIRLS WHO ROCKED THE SCIENTIFIC WORLD GIRLS WHO ROCKED GIRLS WHO ROCKED THE SCIENTIFIC WORLD GIRLS WHO ROCKED THE

Brainy Babes

Joanna Karczmarek

PHYSICIST
(1975 –)

Joanna read the article nervously. Every few paragraphs, she checked her calculations. So far, so good. Holding her breath, she quickly scanned to the end. It worked! Scientists in Ontario had tried an experiment based on her calculations, and it had worked! Her computer simulations, her pencil scratches, her ideas and theories were right.

When Joanna immigrated to Canada from Poland at seventeen, she was already a science buff. She completed her last few years of high school in Ontario, and quickly made a big impression on her teachers, earning amazing results in several math and science competitions. In one, she competed against 5200 students from across Canada in a two-hour exam, and finished in third place.

Joanna also won a physics competition that earned her a spot in the Canadian Physics Olympiad. About twenty students from across the country were invited to a week-long competition and training camp, where they spent hours in lecture halls and laboratories. At the end of the week, Joanna and four other students were selected to represent Canada in the inter-

In the 1700s, Italian Laura Bassi studied math, philosophy, and science — not the usual subjects for a woman. At twenty, she was named the first female professor in the history of the University of Bologna.

national olympiad. Joanna was the first girl ever to earn a place on the team. At the competition in Beijing, China, she won a bronze medal for her work.

With an amazing high school career behind her, Joanna enrolled at Queens University and applied for the Women in Engineering and Science Program. Sponsored by the National Research Council of Canada, the program allowed women to work with scientists in the field for three summers.

During one of her work terms, Joanna met Paul Corkum and the researchers at the Steacie Institute for Molecular Sciences. They had some ideas about lasers and molecules, and they suggested that Joanna help with a theory. For hours and hours, Joanna studied light particles and energy currents. In the end, she and the team of scientists theorized a way to control the spinning of molecules.

A chlorine molecule is made of two atoms, held together by a bond that acts like a rubber band. By precisely aiming pulsing lasers, the researchers thought they could control the spinning of a molecule. Then, by spinning it faster and faster, they could break the "rubber band" within, separating the atoms. Joanna took the theory and created a computer model to help test it. Now, the research team could simulate the results of their ideas.

The team's theory was so impressive that their paper was published in a prestigious scientific journal, and Joanna's name was listed with those of the other researchers — an amazing achieve-

FAST FACT

When the researchers aimed lasers at the molecules, some of the pulses lasted only a few trillionths of a millisecond!

ment for a student. Scientists at the National Research Council painstakingly began to test the theory.

By the time the results came in, Joanna had finished her degree at Queens and was working on her doctorate at Princeton University in the United States. But she was thrilled to hear that the experiment was a success. Her ideas were correct, opening the door to new theories, new science, and new invention.

FOR MORE INFORMATION
http://focus.aps.org/v3/st24.html

Hayoung, age 11

HOW WILL YOU ROCK THE WORLD?
I would like to become a dentist and help my family, because they have a lot of toothaches. I would also like to be a scientist so that I can make new inventions and help the world!

Emily Jennings Stowe

TEACHER, PRINCIPAL, AND PHYSICIAN (1831-1903)

Emily Jennings Stowe and Jennie Trout stepped into the lecture hall, heads held high. They were the first women ever to attend the University of Toronto's medical classes and the male students and professors found new ways each week to shock or embarrass them, hoping the women would quit. But for Emily and Jennie, this was the battle of a lifetime. There was no way they would give up.

Still, it was hard to stifle a scream when they saw their seats. Someone had taken the hands from a cadaver — a body used for medical research — and placed them on the women's chairs. When Emily gasped, the lecture hall roared with laughter. Glaring, she gingerly lifted the hand from her seat and sat down. Jennie did the same.

Emily had been born in 1831 in what is now Ontario. She was raised by her parents, former Quakers, to believe that men and women were equal — a startling belief for the times. By the time she was fifteen, Emily was teaching in the local Norwich school. In search of further education, she applied to the University of Toronto. She was turned down. The school didn't allow female students.

Undefeated, Emily attended teacher's college and, by age twenty, she was the principal of Brantford's public school and the first female principal in Canada.

In 1856, at age twenty-five, Emily married a carriage maker named John Stowe. Married women didn't teach, so Emily gave up her job to care for John and the three children that soon arrived. But when John caught tuberculosis and grew too sick to work, something had to be done. Emily found work at a nearby private school that was less strict about married women teaching. She earned half the wages of the male teachers.

Frustrated by her treatment at the school and bored with her classes, Emily made a bold decision. Returning home one day, she announced to her family that she was going to medical school. Saving every spare penny for tuition, she applied to the University of Toronto, which again turned her down. There were still no women allowed.

Recruiting her sister to care for the children, Emily travelled to the United States to attend the New York Medical College for Women. She graduated in 1867 and when she opened her clinic in Toronto, she became the first Canadian woman to practise medicine in Canada.

Emily's clinic was always busy. Tired of the poor treatment they received from some male doctors, and more comfortable with a woman,

GIRLS AROUND THE WORLD

Florence Nightingale was born into a rich English family and was expected to marry a man from good society. But after touring a hospital in her teens and seeing the horrible conditions there — the nurses were drunk! — Florence decided on a different path. At sixteen, she began visiting the sick. She later attended nursing school in Germany and worked in hospital sanitation and care. At one hospital where she worked, the death rate dropped from forty-two percent to two percent in only a few months.

patients flocked to Emily's examining room. But a new law in Canada required all doctors trained in the United States to complete at least one semester of classes at a Canadian medical school and to write Canadian medical exams. Unfortunately for Emily, no Canadian medical school would admit female students.

Her choices were to give up her practice or continue without a medical licence. Emily refused to give up. She was fined. She was threatened with prison time. The Ontario College of Physicians and Surgeons stood against her. Emily's clinic remained open illegally for thirteen years.

Finally, Emily and one other woman, Jennie Trout, were allowed to attend a semester of classes at the University of Toronto, on one condition. They were not allowed to complain. In classes, they met more harassment than ever before. Students left obscene messages on the blackboards before class. Professors gave lewd lectures designed to embarrass them. After one particularly disgusting lecture, Emily marched up to the professor. "Doctor," she said firmly, "if you continue to lecture in this way, I will be repeating every word of what you say to your wife." That professor didn't bother the women again, and Emily and Jennie continued to ignore the students' taunts until they both successfully finished the term. Emily was finally granted a licence to practise medicine in 1880.

But her fight wasn't over. Angered by the powerlessness of the women she treated, she started the Toronto Women's Suffrage Club, a group that fought for women's rights. They campaigned for improved working conditions and wages, they lobbied the universities to admit women, and they demanded the right to vote.

Some of their campaigns were successful. In 1883, Emily's daughter Augusta became the first woman to receive a medical degree in Canada.

She went on to teach at the newly formed Women's Medical College in Ontario.

Although Emily Stowe died in 1903, due to the continuing work of women's rights groups Ontario women won the right to vote in 1917.

FOR MORE INFORMATION

www.nlc-bnc.ca/women/ewomen1f.htm

Renee, age 12

HOW WILL YOU ROCK THE WORLD?

I would like to do many things, starting with finding a cure for cancer. I would also like to design a luxury car, be a model, an actress, design my own line of clothing (Talerikos), be a cell biologist, be a dentist, be a doctor, and be a director for movies.

Wendy Sloboda

**PALAEONTOLOGICAL
TECHNICIAN
(1968 -)**

As Wendy wandered through the hills of the Milk River Ridge near Warner, Alberta, she kept a close eye on the ground. Wendy's family loved to hunt fossils, and she was used to scouting for them whenever she could. The nineteen-year-old had just finished a summer job with a team of geologists, who had given her several fossil-finding tips.

It was because of one of those tips that she stopped when she saw a tiny piece of black among the rocks. Could it be what she thought? Slowly and carefully, she lifted the flake from the surrounding soil. The black stone that had caught her eye was very thin — about the thickness of a chicken eggshell. It was rough and bumpy, and black. Wendy thought — she hoped — that it might be a fossilized piece of dinosaur eggshell.

As she continued to explore the hillside, she found more and more black chips nestled among the other stones. Collecting several pieces, Wendy packaged them in a container and sent them off to a family friend, geologist Dr. Len Hills at the University of Calgary. He forwarded them to Dr. Philip Currie at the Royal Tyrrell Museum of Palaeontology for analysis.

Wendy didn't have to wait long. She had found more eggshell chips in one spot than had ever been found in all of Canada. Within three days, the museum had a field crew in the area, searching for more pieces. And Wendy was invited to work alongside them. For weeks they combed the area. Millions of years ago, this land had been a tropical swamp. Where would fossils have drifted in the years between? At first,

there were no more discoveries. Then, after a month of searching, success! Not only did they find eggshells, but they found shells with tiny, unborn, duckbilled dinosaurs fossilized within!

In the world of palaeontology, Wendy was an instant star. And her discovery encouraged her to go further. Soon, she became a professional palaeontological technician. Her job? To discover fossils — some of them seventy-five million years old — clean and prepare them, and send them to museum researchers for analysis.

Wendy has been part of many more exciting discoveries. Once, she was walking with a world-renowned palaeontologist looking for dinosaur footprints. Is it possible, she asked, to find an impression of a dinosaur's skin

HOW WILL YOU ROCK THE WORLD?
I want to become an archaeologist and find something to do with aliens or something that explains our history in a phenomenal way.

Alison, age 14

within a footprint? The palaeontologist shook his head. It had never been done. The chances were extremely rare.

The next day, Wendy found a block of sandstone with six footprints on the surface. And one showed skin impressions! The footprints themselves were amazingly well preserved. By studying them, the scientists could tell that the dinosaur had taken a few steps, bent to take a drink, stood, turned, and walked away.

On another dig, Wendy discovered nine bones from a single pterosaur. A few bones from this flying dinosaur had been discovered in the past, but never from the same animal. And one of Wendy's finds was a hand bone. Stuck inside was the fossilized tooth of a theropod — a small meat-eating dinosaur. The small dinosaur must have been chewing on the carcass of the pterosaur.

One of Wendy's discoveries in 1998 made headlines. Working in Eastend, Saskatchewan, she found a forty-three-centimetre-long fossilized piece of dinosaur dung! It was full of crunched-up pieces of bone from other dinosaurs. Since then, scientists have identified the dung — it's from the legendary *Tyrannosaurus rex*.

Wendy continues to hunt the hills for dinosaur fossils. She says she's successful because she knows where to look, and she loves her job. Even when she's not working, her eyes are constantly scanning the ground for new discoveries.

FOR MORE INFORMATION
www.dinosaurvalley.com/kidzone2.html

HOW WILL YOU ROCK THE WORLD?
When I grow up I want to be a veterinarian.
I love animals and I would like to travel around
the world to save them.

Nicky, age 10

Maude Abbott

PHYSICIAN AND SCIENTIST
(1869 – 1940)

Maude looked around her grandmother's home thoughtfully. Her grandmother was over seventy and would need more and more help in the coming years. Maude knew she should be home to take care of her. Still, the seventeen-year-old yearned for more education. Finally, she decided just to ask. "Grandmother," she said, "may I be a doctor?"

In 1886, not many grandmothers would have responded as Maude's did. She merely smiled at Maude and said, "Dear child, you may be anything you like."

Maude had been born in 1869 in St. Andrews East, Quebec. Before she was born, her father was accused of murdering his invalid sister. Her body had been found floating in a river near their home. He was eventually found not guilty, but the shame of the incident drove him away and he abandoned his family. Maude's mother died of tuberculosis, leaving Maude and her older sister Alice in the care of their grandmother.

The two girls were educated at home by a governess, but Maude dreamed of going away to school. In her diary, she made promises to herself. If she could go to school, she would study hard. She would try not to be competitive. She would concentrate on education, not fun.

She got her wish. She attended a small private school in Montreal and won a scholarship to McGill University.

McGill allowed its first female students in 1884. When Maude entered two years later, she was placed in a class with nine intelligent and determined women. Between them, they won three of five medals in their final year. Maude was elected class valedictorian.

Maude was determined to take her education even further, but she needed more than her grandmother's permission. McGill refused her application, allowing no women into its medical school. Bishop's College offered her a place in its classes, but she would also need to attend hospital workshops, and the hospital doctors barred her. They had allowed one woman the year before, but with more applications coming in, they were worried. These female doctors could be competition, taking patients and fees from the men.

Luckily for Maude, some of the hospital's influential supporters heard about her plight. They didn't know Maude, but they could see the situation was unfair. Together, they refused to donate money to the hospital until Maude was allowed in. Her acceptance ticket suddenly arrived in the mail.

Maude graduated with honours in 1894, and went on to postgraduate work in Vienna, Austria. When she returned, she opened a practice in Montreal and began researching heart murmurs for the Royal Victoria Hospital. When her mentor, Dr. Charles Martin, presented her research to the Medico-Chirurgical Society, the society was so impressed that they immediately voted to admit women. Maude became their first female member. Another paper of Maude's was presented in London, England, to great acclaim.

Noting her growing reputation overseas, McGill finally began to recognize Maude's skills. In 1898, the university appointed her curator of the medical museum. The museum materials were in chaos, and Maude began to painstakingly organize and catalogue them, creating a system that could easily be used for research and teaching. She also formed an international association of medical museums, allowing doctors to share information.

Despite her achievements, Maude continued to meet discrimination. McGill refused to appoint her as a full professor, even after other esteemed universities had offered her positions. She was paid less than male teachers, and repeatedly met with resistance to advancement.

Maude ignored these obstacles and published more than 104 research papers. She was eventually granted an honourary doctorate from McGill. She died in 1940, an inspiration to female doctors and medical researchers in Canada and around the world.

FOR MORE INFORMATION
http://library.usask.ca/herstory/abbott.html

Laura, age 10

HOW WILL YOU ROCK THE WORLD?
I'd like to be a doctor (because I like to help people), a lawyer, or a famous baseball player (because I have been taking baseball for five years and this year I'm in triple A!)

Larissa Vingilis-Jaremko

STUDENT
(1982 -)

Nine-year-old Larissa sat at the conference table, listening seriously to the women around her. Larissa's mom was the president of the Canadian Association for Women in Science (CAWIS) and she had invited her daughter to a meeting. Around the room sat biologists and astronomers, university professors and physicists.

When Larissa's mom had invited her, the girl had expected to sit quietly in the background. But the women were soon asking her questions. What did she think of science? What kinds of science did she study in school? What did she think of the issues the association was discussing? Suddenly, the meeting was a fascinating place, full of women who would become role models.

Larissa had always been interested in science. To her, it was a part of daily life. Her father was an engineer and when she asked him why the dining room chandelier shone rainbows on the wall, he explained how prisms divided light into different colours. When she asked her mother about biology, she soon found a microscope on the kitchen table. To Larissa, this wasn't necessarily science — this was just a useful way to learn about the world.

That's why she was so surprised when none of the girls in her grade four class were interested in science. It was boring, they said. Larissa had to admit, the science text-book was a bit of a snooze. And when the class did experiments, the boys did the interesting parts while the girls wrote down the results. Larissa's friends said science was for boys.

She knew that wasn't true. Through her mom, she'd met amazing female scientists. There had to be a way to show the girls in school that science was fun and that anyone could do it. With her parents' help, Larissa drafted an appeal to girls who were interested in forming a science club. She posted it in the CAWIS newsletter. Before long, supportive responses were pouring in — but all from women. There were no replies from girls. Next, Larissa asked some of the scientists she'd met to speak to her class. That was fun, but it didn't make enough of a difference to satisfy her.

When she moved from Toronto to London, Ontario, in grade six, Larissa continued her search for ways to make science interesting. She attended a science and engineering camp that summer and copied out the names and addresses of all the other girls who attended. Then she sent them applica-tion forms, asking them to join a girls' science club.

Soon, Larissa's new organization — the Canadian Association of Girls in Science (CAGIS) — had thirty members. At the first meeting, the girls visited a microbiologist at work. Using microscopes, they examined swamp water, microbes, and glow-in-the-dark bacteria.

The London-based club continued to grow, and at each meeting the members would visit the workplace of a different woman in science. They watched videos of orthopaedic surgery, then performed an operation on a rubber knee. (It's a good thing it was fake, because they accidentally cut the tendon rather than repairing it!)

At other meetings, the group visited a wind tunnel to see aerodynamics in action. They tested bridges and buildings for their resistance to earthquakes. They made their own telescopes, examined the planets, and saw ancient bones at an archaeological site.

FAST FACT

CAGIS has chapters across Canada, and new ones are starting all the time. Check out the website to find the group nearest you or start your own chapter.

Larissa's association was a huge success. In 1995, the teen earned an honourable mention at the Michael Smith Awards for Science Promotion. She was later named a Young Woman of Distinction by the YMCA-YWCA of London.

Today, CAGIS has chapters in Ontario, New Brunswick, Alberta, and British Columbia. And a grant has allowed the association to prepare starter kits for new chapters, now opening across the country.

What's new with Larissa? She's still the founding president of CAGIS and she's busy working on ways to improve the organization. She's also making plans for her future. She's not sure whether she'll ever become a scientist, but that was never the point. She wanted to prove that you don't have to be a boy, a geek, or a genius to love science.

FOR MORE INFORMATION

publish.uwo.ca/~cagis/about.htm

GIRLS WHO ROCKED TO THEIR OWN DRUMMERS

Great Girl Achievements

Sarah Emma Edmonds

SPY
(1841-1898)

Emma packed quickly and quietly. She took a pair of her father's pants, two of his shirts, and a couple of jackets. She pulled a broad-brimmed hat over her forehead, and tucked a Bible under one arm. Surely no one would stop a travelling Bible salesman.

Disguised, Emma slipped from her New Brunswick town before her father realized she was gone. She had spent most of her life trying to please him. The youngest of six daughters, she had done everything she could to make up for the lack of a son. She learned to work hard, shoot well, and ride far better than her sisters. But when her father arranged a marriage to an elderly farmer, she rebelled. There was no way she was getting married.

Once out of town, Emma became Franklin Thompson. She travelled throughout the Maritimes and the United States. On one of her trips, she found herself near the front lines of the American Civil War.

Always looking for adventure, "Franklin" signed on as a male nurse. She was noted for bravery, caring for those wounded in some of the war's

GIRLS AROUND THE WORLD

When she was twelve, Indira Gandhi helped smuggle the records of India's independence party to safety, and organized children's groups to aid the movement. She was later elected India's prime minister, becoming the first woman in the world to lead a democracy in 1966.

fiercest battles. She hunted for fresh food for her patients and, at one point, was almost shot by a grief-stricken woman.

At some point, Emma fell in love with a man she knew from New Brunswick. When he was killed in the war, she applied for the most dangerous position she could think of — a Union spy.

When Emma applied, doctors carefully examined the shape of her head. At the time, many thought the shape of your head showed your character. Luckily, the doctors never thought to examine the shape of Emma's body!

To prepare for her first mission, Emma shaved her hair, bought a black wig, dyed her skin black with silver nitrate, and donned the rough clothes of a slave. She crossed enemy lines in the night, and attached herself to a group of slaves building fortifications. While the others rested, Emma quickly sketched the defences.

The next day, Emma found a job carrying water to the soldiers. If she worked slowly, she could catch pieces of conversation between the officers. She scribbled notes of their conversations.

Emma had a few close calls behind enemy lines. Once, she heard a slave say, "Darned if that fellow ain't turning white." Thinking quickly, Emma told them that her mother was white — she had always expected to turn white sometime. They didn't believe her, but they laughed hard enough for her to make an escape. She quickly added more silver nitrate to her skin.

On the third day of her mission, Emma was posted at the edge of the fortifications, with instructions to shoot enemies on sight. She waited until it began to rain, and the guards on either side took shelter in the trees. Then she crept back towards the Union troops.

That was the first of a dozen missions. She posed as a peddler, a clerk, and the grieving friend of a soldier, bringing back a wealth of information.

But on one of her missions, Emma brought back malaria. Worried that the doctors would discover she was a woman, she deserted from the army.

Emma later revealed her true identity and in 1864 she wrote her autobiography, first titled *Unsexed; or the Female Soldier*. Her book makes it clear that the reason for her disguise as a man was not merely a love of adventure. She wanted access to opportunities that women of the time didn't have.

Years later, when Emma's army superiors were told of her real identity, they praised her intelligence and her courage. As a man or a woman, Emma had been an excellent soldier.

FAST FACT

Emma wasn't the only female spy in the Civil War. Some women were known for gaining information by seducing enemy officers.

FOR MORE INFORMATION

www.wvhc.com/eedmonds.htm

civilwar.bluegrass.net/SpiesRaidersAndPartisans/sarahemmaedmonds.html

Brittany, age 11

HOW WILL YOU ROCK THE WORLD?

I want to ride on the Zamboni at a hockey game because I always thought they were really "cool" (pardon the pun). I also want to jump out of an airplane with a snowboard on and with a parachute!

Viola Huggard MacMillan

PROSPECTOR
(1903 – 1993)

I t was unheard of for a woman to enter Ontario's silver mines. But Viola's brother, proud of his new job, dressed his seventeen-year-old sister in an old pair of overalls and spirited her into the depths of the operation.

She was fascinated. Less than three years later, she had taught herself everything she could about geology, and convinced her new husband to travel to northern Ontario with her, in search of their fortune. For the next ten years, the couple spent most of their time in the bush, facing the threats of weather and wild animals.

Prospecting in northern Ontario was a combination of skill and espionage. Con artists were quick to try to swindle people out of valuable land, and Viola and her husband occasionally staked claims at night to escape notice. Eventually, one of their mines struck gold — literally!

FAST FACT

Viola was one of fifteen children. She quit school to work on the family farm after her brothers left home to fight in World War I.

The small claim that became the Hallnor gold mine earned $53 million. By the 1930s, Viola and her husband owned stakes across the country, and oversaw the operation of countless mines.

Despite being one of only a few female prospectors, Viola was recognized as a natural leader. In the mid-1940s, she was named president of the Prospectors and Developers Association. When she took the post, there were about 100 members. Forty years later, more than 4000 people followed her as she transformed a small, scattered group of companies into a powerful industry.

GIRLS AROUND THE WORLD

Victoria Woodhull was born in Ohio in 1838. In their teens, she and her sister supported themselves as psychics in their parents' travelling show. With the backing of a wealthy financier, the two later became the nation's first female bankers and stockbrokers. The money they earned allowed them to finance a newspaper, which they used to promote Victoria as a presidential candidate. She didn't win, but her campaign made a stir — this was decades before American women won the right to vote.

But Viola's rise to fame was threatened in 1967 when she was convicted of fraud. At the time, it was common for companies to pretend that their stocks were active on the market — something called "wash-trading." Viola's company did the same. The authorities chose her as an example, and sentenced her to nine months in prison.

Viola served only six weeks, and eventually, in 1978, she was pardoned. She was later inducted into the Canadian Mining Hall of Fame, and donated $1.25 million to the Canadian Museum of Nature, in part to help purchase a prized collection of minerals.

At age ninety, Viola was awarded the Order of Canada, praised for her leadership and her position as a role model for women in the mining industry.

FOR MORE INFORMATION

www.geocities.com/Wellesley/9854

Eleanor (Ella) Johnson

REPORTER
(1875 – 1950)

Ella buttoned a collared shirt, donned a man's necktie, and pulled on a sensible tweed skirt and sneakers. In this practical but unconventional outfit, she could chase down a news story as well as any man. Or better. As the marine and financial reporter for *The Vancouver Sun*, Ella knew the docks and shipyards of Vancouver like no one else. She could sniff a news story before it happened, and follow it with unwavering determination.

Ella's career as a reporter began when she was still a teenager. Most women who wrote for newspapers at the time concentrated on fashion or etiquette, but Ella convinced the editor of *The World* — the paper that later became *The Vancouver Sun* —

FAST FACT

Police discovered five small keys among Ella's possessions after she died. No one ever found the safety deposit boxes the keys might unlock.

that she could cover district news. Many of the men in the department objected, but Ella simply ignored them. She made herself a well-known face from the streets of Chinatown to the chambers of City Hall. In one of her best stories, just after the end of World War I, she revealed that the United States was no longer part of an alliance with the Japanese and British navies. With information from a Japanese official, Ella was the first person in the world to announce the news.

When she tired of the newspaper business, Ella bought a taxi in Victoria and became the first female taxi driver in the province. Passengers occasionally tried to cause trouble, but once she showed them the monkey wrench she kept in the front seat for protection, they left her alone. Ella was strong and athletic. She loved swimming, and once swam from Kitsilano Beach to West Vancouver.

Taxi driving wasn't the only "man's" job she tried. She worked in logging, real estate, and insurance before returning to *The Vancouver Sun*. She

GIRLS AROUND THE WORLD

About the same time Ella was digging for stories at the docks, an American woman was building her photo journalism career. Born in 1921 in Wisconsin, Esther Bubley left home in her teens to study photography in Minneapolis. She landed her first big job at *Vogue* magazine at age nineteen. Esther is best known for her work during World War II, when she travelled across the United States capturing images of the country at war.

Linda, age 11

HOW WILL YOU ROCK THE WORLD?

When I grow up, I would like to be the richest businesswoman ever. This goal would be hard to achieve because boys still have the upper hand and get picked for offices first.

ran for office with the Liberals and, when she was badly beaten, she threw her support behind other Liberal politicians. At a time when most women kept their political opinions to themselves, Ella never hesitated to speak.

In 1941, Ella suddenly disappeared from Vancouver. She sold her house and her car, and told her friends that she was going to the Mayo Clinic in the United States for surgery. No one could find any sign of her until she was caught on a Mexican newsreel. Friends were positive they could see her among the crowds in Mexico City.

Ella never returned to Vancouver. In 1951, a hotel manager in Arizona found a dead woman in one of his rooms, and called the police. The woman turned out to be Ella, travelling under the name Edna Jepson. She died of natural causes, and no one ever discovered how she spent the last ten years of her life.

Despite the mystery surrounding her death, Ella's work and her determination to follow her own rules in life inspired many female reporters who followed her into the field.

Tory, age 13

HOW WILL YOU ROCK THE WORLD?
In the next twenty years, I would like to achieve my goal of creating a television show about girls, for girls, and by girls. It will be written, directed, produced, and created by girls.

Kateri Tekakwitha

BLESSED VIRGIN
(1656 - 1680)

Kateri Tekakwitha's aunt sat down beside her. "We've arranged a marriage for you," she said. "He's a young man..." But without waiting to hear about the qualities of her suitor, Kateri shook her head. She would not marry.

Kateri's aunt grew firm. "Your uncle is getting old," she said. "It is time for you to have a husband to help him."

That was a strong argument. Kateri loved her uncle, and hated to hurt him. But she had become a Christian. To her, that meant she had dedicated her life only to God.

Kateri had been born in 1656 to the Algonquin people in what is now Ontario. When she was four, her parents and her baby brother died in a smallpox epidemic. Kateri was attacked by the disease as well. She lost much of her sight, and she would bear scars on her face and limbs for the rest of her life. But she survived.

The young girl was adopted by two aunts and her uncle, chief of the Turtle clan of the Iroquois people. She spent most of her childhood in his village, helping cultivate corn, squash, and beans, cooking cornmeal, and caring for the younger children.

There were three kinds of white men who visited Kateri Tekakwitha's village: soldiers, traders, and missionaries, called black robes by Kateri's people. The black robes came with small gifts, and asked the chief if they could speak with the people about their God.

The chief of Kateri's village agreed and over the next decade the black robes came often. But though the people were hospitable, building the black robes a home within the village, they did not believe their religious teachings.

So when Kateri began to wonder about the stories of the black robes and began to learn more about their religion, she was hesitant to tell her uncle. She

GIRLS AROUND THE WORLD

When Shawnadithit was a child in the early 1800s, she saw her people die. Some were killed by disease, but many of Newfoundland's Beothuk people were slaughtered by European explorers and settlers. Shawnadithit was captured when she was twenty-three, and lived to be the last woman of her race. She taught the European newcomers a little about her culture before she died in 1829.

waited until she was completely sure. Meanwhile, she became more and more adept at avoiding her aunts' plans for marriage.

When Kateri was eighteen, a missionary named Father Jacques de Lamberville arrived in her village. Soon, she made her final decision and asked him to baptize her. After that, life in the village became more and more difficult. Because Kateri wouldn't work on Sundays, her family refused to give her food on that day. They began to give her the worst jobs, and one young man decided to attack her, hoping to scare her out of her "silly" new beliefs.

When the treatment of her people became too harsh, the missionaries helped Kateri escape to the village of Caughnawaga on the St. Lawrence

River, home of other Christian native people. There, Kateri would rise every morning at four and stand in front of the church doors until they opened. She would stay until the last mass was over. In the afternoons, she spent her time in prayer and penitence. She helped the village gather food and she cared for the sick. But her health, never strong, slowly grew worse. She died on April 17, 1680.

Kateri was surrounded by friends and missionaries when she died, and they noticed something strange. Kateri's smallpox scars had stayed with her for life. In death, they seemed to suddenly fade away. Her skin looked smooth. To the missionaries, it was a miracle.

Today, pilgrims visit Kateri's grave in Caughnawaga. The church declared her venerable — a step towards sainthood — in 1943. In 1980, she was beatified, or declared blessed, by Pope John Paul II — a second step. She is the first First Nations person to have been declared blessed.

For girls today, Catholic or not, Kateri is an inspiration. She followed her own beliefs despite opposition and persecution, choosing a path far from ordinary.

FOR MORE INFORMATION

www.catholic.org/saints/saints/kateritekakwitha.html
www.newadvent.org/cathen/14471a.htm

HOW WILL YOU ROCK THE WORLD?
I would like to help homeless people and give them money. It would be for free, so when they are older and they have lots of money, they don't have to pay me back unless they want to.

Mary, age 11

Helen Gregory MacGill

JOURNALIST AND JUDGE
(1864-1947)

C lassical music swelled and glasses clinked at the ball where sixteen-year-old Helen made her debut. She was bedecked in white gloves and a formal gown with a full skirt and slightly ruffled sleeves. She wore flowers in her hair. This was her official introduction to Hamilton's society. From this day forward, she would receive her own invitations to balls, receptions, and dinner parties — events where her parents hoped she would find an eligible husband.

Helen had been born into Hamilton's upper circles in 1864. Her grandfather was a judge and her parents were respected members of the community. Like many girls of her status, Helen attended a private girls' school. And like many girls, she finished school at thirteen, ready to apply herself to learning music, art, proper dress, and housekeeping — skills that would help her as she moved in society.

So it was a surprise when, at nineteen, Helen announced that she would like to become a concert pianist. Her father was not at all sure that this was a respectable career for a woman, but after a lot of persuasion, he took Helen to audition for a well-known instructor, Arthur Fisher. Fisher admitted her immediately, and she began her study.

The men under Fisher's watchful eye were often preparing for entrance to Trinity College. Why, thought Helen, shouldn't she do the same? Trinity allowed women in its classes, although they could receive only certificates, not degrees. Helen took the entrance exams in 1884, and received first-class honours.

But once she was in, Helen decided that she would like a degree, not just a women's certificate. With the help of her grandfather — now seventy-eight — she made her arguments, and the board ruled in her favour. She was now Trinity's first female undergraduate, and on her way to becoming the first woman in the British Empire to receive a music degree.

GIRLS AROUND THE WORLD

Women today are still active in politics and human rights around the world. In Burma, Aung San Suu Kyi had been interested in politics since her childhood. She led opposition to the country's dictatorship, won an election, and was then refused her place in government and held under house arrest. She won the Nobel Peace Prize in 1991 for her peaceful pursuit of democracy, but remains under house arrest.

When Helen finished college, her parents hoped she was back on the path towards marriage. But a chance meeting with an editor in New York offered other opportunities. Soon, Helen was working as a journalist, covering stories in Ontario, the Prairies, Vancouver, and even Japan. On one of her trips, she met Lee Fletcher. The couple married and moved to San Francisco, where Lee went to medical school. Tragically, Lee died young. A hysterical patient cut him with a scalpel, causing a blood infection.

Helen returned to journalism during his illness, this time concentrating on politics. Her stories of government corruption in Minnesota prompted an official investigation. And when new laws were considered, Helen was invited to speak to the legislature. While all of this was taking place, Helen also managed to earn a master's degree.

FAST FACT

The year Helen became a judge was the year women won the right to vote in British Columbia.

She moved to Vancouver and remarried. There she was a founding member of a women's press club (something that had previously only existed for men), and a free nursery, where working mothers could safely leave their children.

Along with some friends, she founded the University Women's Club of Vancouver. At one of the club's meetings, they invited a lawyer to speak on women in the law, and they were shocked to learn how few rights women had. They set out to educate the public and lobby the government, and they had some success. In 1912, a new reform allowed women to practise law.

Five years later, Helen became British Columbia's first female judge. She continued to campaign for women's rights. Her work inspired many of British Columbia's young women, including her daughter Elsie, born in 1905 to Helen and her second husband. Despite having polio in her early twenties, Elsie became the first Canadian woman to earn an electrical engineering degree. She went on to be the first woman in North America to achieve a degree in aeronautical engineering and became the world's first female aircraft designer.

FOR MORE INFORMATION

www.bcarchives.gov.bc.ca/exhibits/timemach/galler10/frames/macgill.html
parkscanada.pch.gc.ca/library/background/71_e.htm

HOW WILL YOU ROCK THE WORLD?
I am going to rock Canada by being a partner in law with my friend Elise. I will also rock Canada by painting, and maybe I will even write in my spare time.

Rebecca, age 10

Acknowledgements

Thank you to the amazing women who took the time to speak to me about their achievements. Thanks also to Min, Gordon, Shirley, Sandy, and Alex for their encouragement and for reading my rough drafts. The help of Heidi, Amber, Mark, and Jeanette in collecting the girls' quotes was invaluable. Beyond Words Publishing deserves credit for a wonderful book concept.

Finally, thanks are due to the many people and organizations that helped me search for information and photographs, including the archives of the City of Vancouver, the City of Victoria, Kamloops, and Salt Spring Island; Florence Hayes and Sherri Stewart at the National Archives of Canada; the State Archives of Michigan; the Hockey Hall of Fame; Maverick Records; the Royal Winnipeg Ballet; *The Toronto Star; The Northern Miner;* and the Royal Tyrrell Museum of Palaeontology.

Photo Credits

SERIOUS SWEAT:

Manon Rheaume: photo courtesy of the Hockey Hall of Fame

Evelyn Hart: photo courtesy of the Royal Winnipeg Ballet

Abby Hoffman: photo courtesy of the National Archives of Canada,
PA 116800

Marilyn Bell: photo courtesy of the National Archives of Canada,
PA 156105

Barbara Ann Scott: photo courtesy of the National Archives of Canada,
PA 112691

Nancy Greene: photo courtesy of the National Archives of Canada,
PA 208679

FRONTIER FEMMES:

Victoria Belcourt Callihoo: illustration by Joanna Clark

Catherine O'Hare Schubert: photo courtesy of the Kamloops Archives,
5817

Madeleine de Verchères: illustration by Joanna Clark

Sylvia Estes Stark: photo courtesy of the Salt Spring Island Archives

Eunice Williams: illustration by Joanna Clark

Esther Brandeau: illustration by Joanna Clark

IN THE LIMELIGHT:

Alanis Morissette: photo courtesy of Maverick Recording

Emily Carr: photo courtesy of the Victoria City Archives, PR73-4963

Emma Albani: photo courtesy of the National Archives of Canada,
PA 149173

Kathleen Parlow: photo courtesy of the National Archives of Canada,
NL 3550

Dorothy Livesay: photo courtesy of the National Archives of Canada,
PA 181514

May Irwin: photo courtesy of the National Archives of Canada, C23092

BRAINY BABES:

Joanna Karczmarek: photo courtesy of *The Toronto Star*/A. Stawicki

Maude Abbott: photo courtesy of the National Archives of Canada,
C9479

Wendy Sloboda: photo courtesy of the Royal Tyrrell Museum of
Palaeontology

Emily Jennings Stowe: photo courtesy of the National Archives of Canada,
C9480

GREAT GIRL ACHIEVEMENTS:

Sarah Emma Edmonds: photo courtesy of the State Archives of Michigan,
02254

Viola Huggard MacMillan: photo courtesy of *The Northern Miner*

Eleanor Johnson: photo courtesy of City of Vancouver Archives, Add. Mss.
396, vol. 3, p. 3

Kateri Tekakwitha: illustration by Joanna Clark

Helen MacGill: photo courtesy of City of Vancouver Archives, N. 1073 #2

Index

About the Author

Tanya Lloyd has spent her first 20 years training for a life of fame and fortune. Unfortunately, *NSYNC rejected her application to be a back-up dancer, her dismal chemistry grade drastically reduced her chances of joining NASA, and she lacked the physical endowments necessary to become a World Wrestling Federation star. At 21, she turned her hand to writing travel books, raving about the beauty of places that she had never actually visited. *Canadian Girls Who Rocked the World* is her first children's book.